PARENTING CHILDREN

WITH

ADHD

"in the USA"

A Practical Guide to Boost Focus, Improve Attention and Raise Happy, Successful Kids Through Strong Loving Relationships

By

Grace S. Anderson

Dear Reader,

You are about to dive into an extraordinary resource that will change the way you approach the challenge of parenting children with ADHD. "Parenting Children with ADHD in the USA: A Practical Guide to Boost Focus, Improve Attention, and Raise Happy, Successful Kids Through Strong Loving Relationships" is a book aimed at providing you with a practical and valuable guide to navigate this complex reality and offer your children a bright future.

The author of this book, Grace S. Anderson, is a prominent socio-pedagogical researcher and one of the leading experts in ADHD, acute and post-traumatic stress in children, learning techniques, and language. With a classical education and a specialization in responding to the ADHD diagnosis of her firstborn, Grace has dedicated herself every day to finding the best tools to disseminate the results of her research and help as many people as possible.

Through her personal experience and academic background, Grace has developed a unique and innovative approach to managing ADHD in children. This book is the result of her unwavering commitment to deeply understanding the challenges faced by parents of children with ADHD on a daily basis. Her mission is to provide the necessary support to face diagnoses that can unsettle parents calmly and with the right tools. Furthermore, her goal is to provide a solid foundation of knowledge and skills that will help parents interpret and understand the diagnosis correctly, preparing them to seek the right help and equip themselves with the necessary skills to assist their child.

"Parenting Children with ADHD in the USA" is not just a theoretical manual but also a companion that will guide you step by step towards a deeper understanding of ADHD and practical solutions to address it. Through advice, strategies, and heartfelt stories, you will discover how to develop positive attitudes and strong relationships with your children, providing them with a loving and supportive environment in which they can grow and thrive.

This book is based on years of high-level research involving prominent figures in the field. Thanks to the collaboration with readers and fellow researchers, the author has had the valuable opportunity to expand the content to meet the specific needs of parents in the United States of America. Additionally, the cover has been modified to accurately reflect the book's true purpose and offer a clear understanding of its content.

Within these pages, you will find a wealth of practical advice, insights, and tools to help you positively and consciously raise your children with ADHD. You will discover strategies to improve attention and concentration, manage challenging behaviors, and promote the development of healthy self-esteem in your children. Furthermore, you will be provided with tangible support to tackle the challenges related to ADHD in the academic, social, and family spheres.

I invite you to read each page carefully, reflect on the concepts presented, and put the proposed strategies into practice. This book will guide you on a journey of discovery and personal growth, offering you a comprehensive framework to confidently and determinedly address ADHD.

It is crucial to recognize that every culture is unique, and as such, their approach to finding solutions and the tools available may differ significantly. Parenting children with ADHD is a challenge that transcends borders and affects families worldwide. While this book is tailored to the specific needs of parents in the United States of America, it is important to acknowledge that experiences and resources may vary across cultures.

Societal norms, educational systems, and support networks play a vital role in shaping parents' strategies and approaches to managing ADHD. The author, Grace S. Anderson, has considered the distinct context of parenting in the United States, incorporating research and insights that specifically address American families' challenges. However, it is essential to recognize that adapting these strategies to your own cultural context may be necessary to achieve the best outcomes for your child.

Are you ready to embark on this path towards more conscious parenting and provide your children with the necessary resources to successfully navigate the challenges of ADHD? Get ready to immerse yourself in the following pages and be inspired by the words of Grace S. Anderson, an authoritative and compassionate voice who will accompany you throughout the entire journey.

Wishing you a fulfilling reading experience!

Dear Parents I'm Grace Anderson and welcome

to the *Extraordinary Opportunity* to be parents of children with Attention Deficit Hyperactivity Disorder (ADHD) who know their children's discomfort and know how to help
them. As an Author and Mother, I have witnessed firsthand the Challenges and Triumphs
that accompany the Education of children with ADHD. It is my sincere belief that Every
child <u>Deserves Tailored Love, Understanding, and Support to Thrive on their unique Journey.</u>

While there are Countless Resources and Strategies to Guide Parents in Managing ADHD,
it is vital to Recognize the importance of Understanding how to walk this path specifically
in the United States. Why? **Because Every Country is Different,** and the United States,
with its rich tapestry of services and diverse cultural landscape, presents its own set of
Opportunities and Obstacles for Parents and their Children with ADHD.

Parents, you are the true Superheroes in your child's Life and your Role in Supporting
and defending them cannot be Underestimated. By gaining knowledge about Managing
ADHD in the US, you are taking the crucial first step in <u>Helping your Children Reach New
Heights.</u>

First of all, understanding the services available to parents is crucial. We are Fortunate
in the United States of America to have a wide variety of resources, from Specialized
Schools and Educational Programs to treatment options and support groups. By delving
into the unique systems and services accessible within the country, you will **Discover a
Wealth of Tools and Approaches to Help your Child's Development.**

Additionally, Culture plays a vital role in shaping our perspectives on parenting and our
children's health. In the United States, Our Society embraces a wide variety of beliefs,
customs, and Expectations. Cultural factors significantly influence how ADHD is perceived, Diagnosed and Managed within our Communities. By Gaining Insight Into the Cultural
Nuances Surrounding **ADHD in the United States,** you can navigate these complexities
with empathy and confidence.

Above all, Dear Parents, I urge you to Recognize the Transformative Power of Knowledge.
By arming yourself with **Specific Information on ADHD Management in the United
States, you Become an Empowered Advocate for your Children.** You can collaborate

effectively with Educators, Health Professionals and Support Networks, ensuring your child receives the tailored support they Need To Thrive.

*** REMEMBER: YOU ARE NOT ALONE ON THIS JOURNEY ***

Together, we can lead the way to a better future for our children with ADHD. By beginning your quest for understanding, you are taking an extraordinary step towards making a lasting difference in the lives of your loved ones.

With Warmth and Admiration,

Author of "Parenting Children with ADHD in the USA"

Grace S. Anderson

TABLE

OF

CONTENT

INDEX

CHAPTER 1

Identify and Understand ADHD

1.1 What is ADHD?

ADHD, a condition that affects many, It can make life challenging, it can make life less zany, It stands for Attention Deficit Hyperactivity Disorder, And it can make focus and attention a bit of a border.

For those who live with ADHD every day, Simple tasks can seem like a disarray, Their minds are constantly racing and jumping around, Making it hard to settle and concentrate, it can astound.

Symptoms may include fidgeting, impulsivity, and distractibility, All of which can make life seem like an impossibility, But with proper understanding and treatment, one can thrive, And live a happy, successful life, taking life's ride.

A youngster with ADHD may have issues at school, with family, or with friends. So let us show compassion and support for those with ADHD, And help them to overcome their obstacles and live life happily, For they have so much to offer and so much to give, And with our love and understanding, they can learn to truly live.

1.2 What is ADD?

It stands for Attention Deficit Disorder and it can be Rough.
 For those who live with ADD every day, simple tasks can seem like an uphill, it can sway.

Their minds may wander and lose focus easily, making it hard to stay on track and follow things breezily. They may struggle with organization and time management all of which can make daily life a bit of an impediment.

But with proper understanding and support, those with ADD can learn to navigate life's court, they can tap into their creativity and unique perspective and find success and fulfillment in ways that are respective

Adults with ADD often struggle with executive skills; miss appointments frequently, have problems concentrating on academic work, and have trouble keeping track of time. Individuals who have these symptoms may have predominantly Inattentive Type ADHD, as it is currently known among doctors. While it is no longer a recognized medical diagnosis, "ADD" is often used to describe specific symptoms in the broader category of "ADHD."

1.3 What ADHD IS NOT?

A misleading and perhaps damaging label is ADHD.

 ADHD is classified as a pathology or illness when referred to as a "deficit disorder". People with ADHD don't have a sickness and they don't have a shortage of attention—instead, they have a surplus of it. Controlling it is a problem.

Thus, we contend that "varying attention stimulus trait" (VAST) is a more appropriate descriptive word. This moniker enables us to "de-medicalize" ADHD and instead emphasise the enormous benefits of utilizing an ADHD brain.

Naturally, VAST symptoms may harm a person's life, career and relationships. Dr William Dodson created the term "rejection sensitive dysphoria," which describes the intense emotional sensitivity and frequent emotions of guilt, humiliation and rejection reported by those with VAST.

Yet, pairings are always there with VAST; you may know hyperfocus before losing concentrate. Being often distracted, you are also naturally curious. So, even while people with VAST tend to crumble under perceived rejection, they may also readily flourish under it, a state we refer to as "recognition-responsive bliss."

1.4 Types of ADHD

The three kinds of ADHD are mostly inattentive, primarily hyperactive plus impulsive, and mixed. Each presentation is identified by a particular collection of behavioural symptoms listed in the DSM-5, which doctors use to diagnose. Learn about these requirements as well as the symptoms' severity ranges here.
There are 3 Types of ADHD:
• Primarily Inattentive ADHD (formerly called ADD)
• Primarily Hyperactive and Impulsive ADHD
• Combined Type ADHD

It used to be known as attention deficit hyperactivity disorder (ADD) or ADHD. Historically, "ADHD" was used to describe impulsive and hyperactive symptoms, whereas "ADD" was used to describe inattentive symptoms, including difficulty listening or time management. According to updates to the Diagnostic & Statistical Manual for Mental Disorders (DSM-V) 1, the disorder is now known as ADHD, and individuals are diagnosed as having 1 of 3 appearances.

Inattentive Type ADHD

Due to their difficulties paying attention over time, adhering to specific directions, and planning tasks and activities, people experiencing inattentive ADHD often make unintentional errors. They often misplace items, have poor working memories, and are quickly distracted by outside stimuli. ADHD, once known as ADD, is more often diagnosed in men and females.

Hyperactive and Impulsive Type ADHD

ADHD sufferers who are hyperactive feel the desire to move all the time. They often wiggle, fidget, and have trouble staying still. Youngsters often behave like they are propelled by the motor and move about a lot. All ages may exhibit excessive talking, interruptions, blubbering out replies, and self-control issues. Men and children are more often diagnosed with this kind of ADHD.

Combined Type ADHD

Six or more inattention symptoms and six or more hyperactive and impulsive symptoms are present in people with combined-type ADHD.

1.5 Identify ADHD

ADHD (Attention deficit hyperactivity disorder) symptoms may be divided into two categories of behavioural issues:

• Impulsivity and over activity
• Inattentiveness (trouble focusing and concentration)

While this is rare, many persons with ADHD have issues that fit into both categories.

For instance, around 2 to 3, out of 10 individuals with the disease struggle with concentration and attention but not hyperactivity or impulsivity.
Attention deficit disorder is another name for this specific kind of ADHD (ADD). Since the signs of ADD may not always be as clear, it occasionally goes undetected.
Boys than females are diagnosed with ADHD more often. Females are less likely to engage in disruptive behaviour, which makes the symptoms of ADHD more pronounced, and are more likely to exhibit signs of inattentiveness. It implies that ADHD in females may not often be recognized.
Children and teens with ADHD often have well-defined symptoms that become apparent by age six. These happen in several settings, including at school and home. Youngsters may exhibit signs of inattention, hyperactivity, and impulsivity, or they may exhibit signs of one of these kinds of behaviour.

1.6 Tools to Identify ADHD

A person who has been diagnosed with ADHD could undergo treatments like:
• Counseling
• Special Education
• Medications
• Psychological Counseling

Although it's conceivable for children with ADHD to have lifelong symptoms, it's also conceivable that they may go away as they become older.
The majority of the time, ADHD is quite controllable, particularly when treated according to a multimodal treatment plan with the help of a mental health specialist.
There are several tools that can be used to identify ADHD, including:

1. Rating scales: these are questionnaires completed by parents, teachers or in-

dividuals with ADHD to assess symptoms and impairment. Examples include the ADHD Rating Scale-5 and the Conners Rating Scales.

2. Neuropsychological testing: this involves a series of tests that assess cognitive abilities, such as attention, memory and executive function. Examples include the Continuous Performance Test and the Wisconsin Card Sorting Test.

3. Behavioral observations: this involves observing the individual in various settings, such as home and school, to assess behavior and social skills.

4. Diagnostic interviews: these are structured interviews conducted by a clinician to gather information about symptoms and impairment. Examples include the Diagnostic Interview Schedule for Children and the Kiddie Schedule for Affective Disorders and Schizophrenia.

5. Brain imaging: This involves using imaging techniques, such as MRI or fMRI, to assess brain structure and function. While not commonly used for diagnosis, brain imaging can provide additional information about the underlying neural mechanisms of ADHD.

CHAPTER 2

Potential Causes of ADHD

While the precise causation of ADHD (attention deficit hyperactivity disorder) is unknown, many variables are believed to be to blame.

Brain structure and function

The special relevance of many potential changes in the brains of persons with ADHD and those without the disorder has not yet been determined by research. For instance, brain scan research has revealed that some brain regions may be smaller and others may be bigger in individuals with ADHD.
Some research has hypothesised that neurotransmitters may be out of balance in the brains of persons with ADHD or may not function correctly.

Genetics

In most instances, it's believed that the genes you acquire from your parents play a key role in developing the disorder since ADHD seems to run in families. According to research, those with ADHD are more prone to have parents or siblings with the disorder.
Nevertheless, the inheritance pattern for ADHD is probably complicated and is not assumed to be caused by a single genetic defect.

Groups in danger

Additionally, some people are thought to be more susceptible to developing ADHD, such as those who were born prematurely before the 37th week of mother's pregnancy or had a low birth weight; those who have epilepsy; and those who have brain damage that either occurred in the womb or as a result of serious head injuries later in life.

2.1 Tips for pregnant

The likelihood that ADHD, as it is more commonly known, may manifest during pregnancy is increasing daily. The increasing exposure to digital gadgets is the primary cause of this. The most prevalent traits are the inability to focus on anything and constant hyperactivity. Some distinct features distinguish this condition. In any situation, people are prone to acting impulsively.
But, the best part is that researchers have identified several potential treatments for ADHD during pregnancy that might help to avoid it.

Purchase the right probiotics for you: The emergence of ADHD during pregnancy is one of the health disorders for which probiotics play a significant role.Providing the essential probiotics to the pregnant woman will not only be helpful for her general health but also encourage the baby's development and growth. Using the proper probiotics not only lowers the risk of developing illnesses like bipolar disorder, autism, mood disorders, and possibly schizophrenia in children but also lo wers the risk of ADHD in neonates.

Consume filtered water: Water that hasn't been filtered includes a lot of pollutants and other unsanitary elements. Drinking unfiltered water should be avoided, particularly throughout your pregnancy.

Limit your sugar intake: One of the key actions you can do to avoid developing ADHD while pregnant is adopting a low-sugar diet. Several studies have shown a clear link between the mother's excessive sugar diet and the child's development of ADHD. It has a very direct cause. That is so since the human body has a gene called IGF2 responsible for the brain's growth. Yet when the diet contains a lot of sugar, your IGF2 levels are harmed, which eventually causes ADHD to appear. Thus, limit your intake of refined proteins and maintain a balanced diet. If required, speak with a dietitian who may provide a suitable eating plan.

Keep your mobile phones away from you: Digital gadgets, in general, have a negative influence on foetuses, which often results in ADHD. Mobile phones undoubtedly play a significant role in your daily life. Still, you may avoid using them when unnecessary by keeping them out of sight, particularly out of your pockets. You must be extremely careful and take all required measures during the weeks of pregnancy while your body is exposed to hazardous external elements to prevent your kid from developing ADHD. Keep your diet, and go to your checks as scheduled.

2.2 Family Influence

Children with ADHD have a poorer household environment than ordinarily developing kids. Children's chances of developing ADHD may be increased by family factors, particularly the parents' emotional instability and lower levels of education and work. Moreover, children with ADHD may interact with negative family contextual variables due to behavioural issues and social functioning deficits. Consequently, early therapies that concentrate on the problematic elements may help enhance the social-behavioural abilities of ADHD youngsters.

2.3 Influence of Education

ADHD may impair a student's capacity for concentration, focus, attention, and effort while completing coursework. A student with ADHD may also get agitated, restless, speak excessively or disturb the class. Children with ADHD may also struggle academically due to learning impairments.

The majority of children with ADHD begin school before receiving a diagnosis. Sometimes, teachers are the first to identify potential ADHD symptoms. With the child's parents, they could discuss it. The parent might then ask a medical professional to assess the kid to determine whether they have ADHD.

An individual with ADHD has a distinct neural network in their brain that operates differently. In many instances of ADHD, the frontal lobe is discovered to be substantially undeveloped. There have also been reports of neurotransmitter-level imbalances. Constant movement, trouble focusing, and irrational conduct are the main characteristics of the disorder.

Many studies have been done to comprehend the patterns, prognosis, and effects of ADHD on development. Much research has investigated the neural reactions to reward, the genotypic connection, and behavioural characteristics of ADHD patients throughout age groups. Also, extensive epidemiological investigations are being carried out for a diverse population sample.

2.4 Influence of the Environment

The results suggest that lifestyle variables may be crucial in developing ADHD.

They demonstrated, in particular, that better planning of activities beyond school hours and ensuring children get enough sleep could have a preventive effect concerning the beginning of ADHD symptoms in youngsters. Lastly, these results pave the way for other avenues of inquiry. Due to the nature of our research, we could not independently analyse the impact of each form of cognitively challenging activity.
As a result, it was impossible to determine which activity had the largest impact, such as whether studying or solving puzzles had a bigger impact.

CHAPTER 3

ADHD Diagnosis: And Now?

3.1 Understand the Diagnosis

A medical examination such as any blood test or X-ray cannot be used to diagnose ADHD. Instead, a medical expert will evaluate you to determine whether you have ADHD.

An expert compiles data during the examination to see if the ADHD criteria are satisfied. The DSM, the recognised diagnostic manual in the United States, serves as the source for the criteria. These tests may be used to identify ADHD in both adults and children.

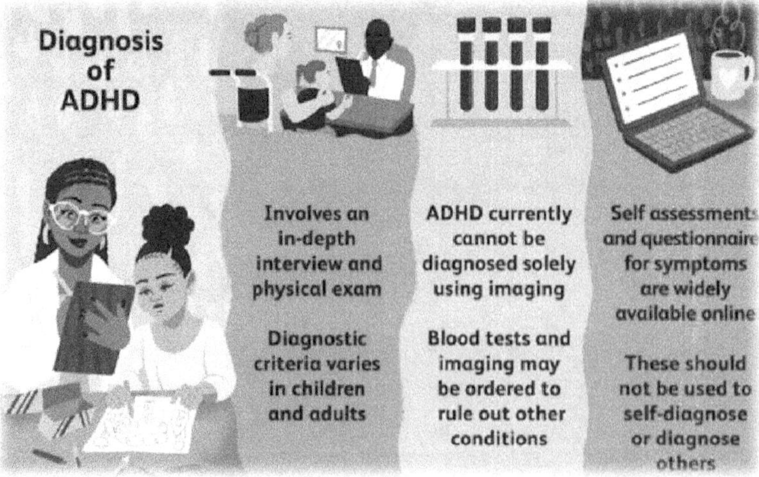

Diagnostic Standards

Inattentive, combined, or hyperactive-impulsive, ADHD is the three basic forms. Regardless of how ADHD manifests specifically, several criteria must be satisfied before an official diagnosis may be made:
• Many signs appear before the age of 12
• Symptoms limit or interfere with regular functioning
• The symptoms appear in many contexts (home, work, school)
• The symptoms cannot be described more appropriately by alternative mental health issue

ADHD evaluations

While assessing for ADHD, certain particular tests may be done, such as:

Conners Rating Scale: Examines behavioural, intellectual, interpersonal, and occupational symptoms to assess how symptoms affect daily living, relationships, and other spheres of one's life; also known as the Conners Adult ADHD Rating Scales are used to measure adult ADHD.

TOVA (Tests of Variable Attention): Used in combination with other evaluations to gauge the capacity to focus on non-favourite activities

NEBA: Health practitioners may also use the Neuropsychiatric EEG-Based Assessment Aid System in addition to self-report and interview-based evaluations. Monitoring brain wave patterns, particularly are often more pronounced in children with ADHD, is required.

BASC (Behavior Assessment System for Children): Examines signs of anxiety, depression, hyperactivity, behaviour problems, and learning difficulties.

CBCL (Child Behavior Checklist or Teacher Report Form): Used to evaluate behavioural and social concerns, including hostility, physical complaints, and withdrawal

ASRS (ADD in adults Self-Report Scale): A questionnaire to assess adult ADHD symptoms.
Children between the ages of six and 17 may take this ADHD exam.

Level of ADHD
A doctor may also specify severity when diagnosing ADHD in a patient:

Moderate: More substantial impairment.

Mild: You or your kid shows a little functional impairment despite exhibiting enough symptoms to match the diagnostic criteria.

Severe: Much more symptoms than would be necessary to diagnose ADHD are present, together with severe impairment brought on by symptoms.

The Value of a Correct Diagnose

There may be a temptation to delay receiving a formal diagnosis for you or your kid. After all, if you don't intend to take medicine, what's the point? Maybe you worry that having a diagnosis of ADHD would do more harm than good.
However, receiving a diagnosis of ADHD has several benefits. You or your kid with a diagnosis may be given the right therapy, which can help rule out all other problems. Autism, sleep disorders, bipolar illness, anxiety disorders, and conduct disorders are all separate diagnoses, even if they might mirror the symptoms of ADHD.

It also has a psychological advantage. ADHD symptoms may make people feel guilty, ashamed, or embarrassed about their academic shortcomings. Alternatively, it might result in much annoyance about how long it takes to do chores. A diagnosis could lessen such feelings.

Although if you don't want to utilise medicine as part of the therapy, receiving a diagnosis might be the first step in seeking support.
Simple adjustments, such as shifting your workstation to a serene location or being given additional time on examinations, may significantly impact.

When you provide formal documentation of a diagnosis, accommodations may be granted at school or the place of employment.
With an ADHD diagnosis, you may start a course of therapy to help you manage your life better.

What Information to Give Your Treatment Provider

Bring copies of any pertinent documents, such as medical, psychiatric, and academic or job records, to the appointment if feasible. Prepare a thorough family and social history in advance.
To finish the consultation, many healthcare professionals may email you a questionnaire. The completed paperwork must be brought along to the appointment.

With your permission, they may also distribute the questionnaire to others, like the child's teacher or childcare provider.

Experts in ADHD Diagnosis

Various specialists are certified to conduct ADHD testing and provide a diagnosis. ADHD may be identified by a neurologist, psychiatrist, psychotherapist, psychologist, or other medical professionals. Inquire about the care provider's expertise in ADHD diagnosis before scheduling an appointment.
You might begin by speaking with your doctor if you're seeking to have your ADHD symptoms evaluated. Your primary care physician may not do the full assessment but can refer you to someone who can do so.
Some paediatricians and family doctors can identify ADHD. You may request an appointment with a specialist for additional evaluation if your doctor feels that you or your kid has ADHD.

Online ADHD assessments are not valid. Yet, there is a tonne of online tests and questionnaires for ADHD that serve as a useful self-screening procedure. After taking a questionnaire, you may feel more comfortable asking a doctor for a proper diagnosis.

The Evaluation Procedure

A normal examination for ADHD in adults or children may span one to three hours. However, this varies. Each practitioner carries out the examination differently, but you can anticipate an in-person consultation covering subjects including development, health, family history, and lifestyle.
The physician may ask to interview other subjects. They may wish to speak with their partners and other family members as grownups. The physician could wish to speak with a coach, teacher, or childcare provider for youngsters.

The evaluation may include questionnaires, behaviour ratings, intellectual tests, and measurements of attentiveness and distractibility.
You can be requested to go into detail on issues like:

• How frequently do you lose things?
• Do you have difficulty staying seated?
• How frequently do your surroundings sidetrack you?
• How frequently do you give up on a project before it's finished?
• How frequently do you forget key dates or events?
• Do you have trouble unwinding?

Your medical background has a significant role in the assessment. It can be advised to have a checkup if you haven't had one lately to rule out any medical explanations for your symptoms.

Whereas psychological testing does not constitute the only way to diagnose ADHD, it may be suggested to confirm findings and provide a more thorough evaluation. The possibility of a learning disability test is also present.

3.2 Manage New Emotions

Emotions are felt more strongly by those with ADHD than by others. They become more intriguing and engaging when they experience joy and excitement. Yet, intense emotion may sometimes be detrimental.

Impulsivity is a symptom of ADHD. They behave without thinking about how their actions may impact others or themselves because they are swept away by their emotions. You can get excited and forget to purchase the other items on your list if you find something intriguing at the store.

Having the proper emotion and experiencing it at the proper intensity is the difficulty of emotional self-control. People having ADHD struggle on both sides of that equation when it relates to task completion.

Distractions thrill them, and they get weary of their intended duties. They are unable to retreat. They're unable to complete tasks. They may ponder, "Why am I always so emotional?"

Daily problems caused by a lack of emotional stability are typical and predictable:

• Behaving impulsively: without pausing to consider one's actions.
• Losing sight of the broader picture might cause them to make poor judgements.
• Uttering a phrase you later come to regret
• Taking a job off the spot
• Sharing excessively: There are moments when it's preferable to keep your mouth shut, such as at a business meeting or while attempting to control a difficult youngster.
• People with ADHD have "motivational deficit disorder," making it more difficult to start and complete uninteresting activities. This illness develops when we give in to our emotions.
• Losing sight of the other person and becoming egotistical or hurting a friend's emotions
• Negatively affecting your boss's, family, or friends' relationships by expressing displeasure or irritation.

3.3 Communicate with the Family

It might be difficult to parent a kid with attention deficit or attention deficit hyperactivity disorder. Communicating is crucial, but it may be challenging when a kid has concentration or sensory issues.
The following tips can help you and your kid communicate more effectively.

Give them concise, straightforward instructions.

Little ones are easily overpowered. Give them step-by-step directions if you're instructing them on anything or requesting them to do a job. Don't, however, list every step in one go. Give kids one or two straightforward stages, and then proceed once each one is finished.

Please provide them with options.

Children rapidly learn to shut out their parents' conversations, particularly when they believe you are speaking to them instead of to them. Giving your kid an option makes it simpler for them to pay attention. They often give themselves permission to take their time and consider their options to make
the best choice possible. Whenever it's time for bed, for instance, you can say, "Time for bed now. Which pair of red and blue pyjamas would you like to wear tonight?"

Be calm and use gentle speech.

Your youngster may get stimulated if you grow irritated or raise your voice. It defeats the purpose of your efforts, particularly if they're already anxious or upset. Keep your cool and speak to your youngster softly. Step aside and participate in a peaceful activity that they could find intriguing if they're yelling or acting upset. Colour, puzzle together or construct a tower out of blocks. Your composure will have an impact on them.

Identify when your youngster is listening to you and focusing on you.

Mostly, individuals need to make eye contact to feel heard. A youngster who has ADD or ADHD, however, has a quick-thinking mind. They could find it difficult to look you in the eye or to keep it open. It doesn't imply that they aren't paying attention. Contrarily, a lot of kids fumble with items while they're listening. Be aware of your child's clues.

Develop communication plans.

While attempting to connect with your kid, you sometimes need to think outside the box. Introduce a "listening ball," for instance! Whereas they listen to you, instruct your youngster to hold a ball or throw this from hand to hand. You may also utilise visual clues to communicate to your kid what you desire or require them to perform. When it's time to bed, give them their stuffed animal or display an image of a bed.

Make use of visuals.

Visual aids are effective for engaging kids with ADD and ADHD. Make a poster with images showing preparing for bed rather than telling them what to do. Describe your objectives.
Children behave better when they are conscious of what is required of them, plus what they may anticipate. Rewarding good conduct encourages collaboration in the future.
Parenting a kid with ADHD calls for some innovative strategies. Discover the clues and triggers of your kid. See how they like to learn, and then use your communication to promote that method.

3.4 Find the Ways Together

Understanding the issue is the first step in finding good solutions. Most of the emotional self-control techniques covered here is founded on three fundamental principles: managing stress, having techniques for restraining your emotions in trigger circumstances and taking responsibility for your responses.

1. Refrain from taking on too much. Up to the point when we realize we have a lot going on, everything appears engaging. By taking on fewer obligations and respectfully cancelling certain commitments when necessary—and with sufficient notice—you may reduce stress during times of stress.

2. Consistently work out. A fantastic way to reduce stress is through exercise. No matter how you workout, as much as you do it often, it doesn't matter. Even a brief stroll around the block or a series of push-ups will help you to relax and put things into perspective.

3. Handle comorbid mood disorders. Anxiety and sadness are more common in adults with ADHD. Handling these issues with professionals is advisable since, if left untreated, they could worsen your emotional control.

4. Have a plan... Preparing in advance on how to react to a circumstance that you are aware of may cause some intense emotions. Consider your options for responding to the other person's actions and the results you want to see. Before entering the scenario, review the strategy, and maintain it in the back of your mind while you are in it. Bring some written notes if you can.

5. Teach people to criticise you. Train several friends and family to speak to you about the larger picture or another person's perspective if you know you will become emotional in definite situations, political debates, or sales at certain stores. It will assist you in recognizing yourself earlier throughout the process of becoming caught up together in feeling.

6. Keep in mind the viewpoint of the other person. We respond to those closest to us. Although we'd all want to believe that our emotions are warranted, there are occasions when we respond to an individual for reasons that aren't related to them. Don't let things that don't directly affect you bother you.

7. Inform people about your emotional tendencies. Tell your family, close friends, and maybe certain colleagues that you sometimes get too emotional at first but that you soon calm down and can have an effective conversation. It aids them in preventing overreaction to your response. Also, you might train them on how you want them to react to you if you experience a powerful emotion.

8. Control your tension. Everyone has moments of tension and exhaustion. Try to restrict the demands placed on you as much as possible.

9. Get enough rest. After we've received enough, we are more optimistic and less reactive.

10. Schedule personal time. Setting aside time for yourself to indulge in something enjoyable is crucial. You will exhaust yourself if you don't replenish the batteries.

11. Keep emotional triggers at bay. A strong response is more difficult to control than trying to prevent it initially. Not every unpleasant or challenging scenario should be avoided, but you should know that some aren't worth the hassle.

12. Have a rest. It is preferable to leave if your two options are to blow something up or stay. You may need only five seconds to relax and collect yourself. Explain to the person you are upset with in a continuing relationship that taking a break will allow you to cool down and provide a better result for everyone.

13. Tell yourself that the emotion you are experiencing will pass no matter how intense. It might be a good sensation, such as excitement about a possible purchase, or a terrible one, such as a disastrous date. While the emotion remains, be aware that it will change.

14. Keep emotion and behaviour distinct. While our emotions often influence our conduct, there need not always be a clear link between the two. It's possible to be aware of your feelings and what causes you to desire but not act on them, even if it's easier said than done. Individuals learn how to achieve this via mindfulness training.

15. After you've calmed down, clarify what you truly meant. Inform the individual of your reasoning and what you intended if anything came across incorrectly or if you mentioned something you didn't mean to. Don't dispute another person's thoughts, but let her understand that your true intentions were better than what came over.

3.5 Understand the Obstacles

Concentrating despite ongoing distractions

For kids in school, attention issues may be particularly challenging. Children with ADHD may quickly be diverted by their surroundings while the instructor speaks. Background sounds might block out the instruction, like the sound of anyone clicking their pen. The child's academic ability and willingness to remain on target may suffer.

School adjustments may be helpful for certain children. The child might take place in a space with minimal work and allocate more time for tasks to compensate for break time.

Remove distractions from environments where you need to concentrate if you have adult ADHD. It can include switching off the phone and finding a quiet area to work in. You may maintain attention by having a tidy workstation that you use solely for work.

Possessing a mind that's too busy

Racing thoughts are particularly common in adults with ADHD, which may cause agitation and sleeplessness since they prevent you from falling asleep.

Your thoughts may seem to be moving at one mile per minute if you have a hyperactive mind. You probably have a lot going through your head, finding it challenging to concentrate on one item at a time.

Stressful thinking might be erratic. Take up some mindfulness training to relax your thoughts. Take a few deep breaths and concentrate on the here and now. You may try reciting a mantra that uplifts you and enables you to concentrate on a single idea, such as "it will be alright."

Skipping or hurriedly consuming meals

It's simple to lose time and discover you skipped a meal when easily distracted. You could then feel hungry, resulting in binge eating or overeating.
To maintain more regular eating patterns, think about the following advice:
Spread out your meals throughout the day and practise being present throughout meals to reduce the likelihood of rushing through them. Avoid distractions at mealtimes, such as browsing on your cellphone or watching TV.
According to studies from 2018, eating issues often coexist with ADHD. If you believe you have an eating issue, consider discussing your choices with a mental health expert.

Having a poor sense of worth

ADHD in children is often misinterpreted. They may get continual criticism for their conduct or attitude because they are perceived as misbehaving or possessing too much energy. It may eventually result in problems with self-esteem.
Adults with ADHD often feel ashamed about feeling as if they fall short of expectations because of attention, focus, and overload problems. It may contribute to or support poor self-esteem.
When low self-esteem hits, practising self-compassion may help you be nice to yourself and embrace yourself just as you are.

Juggling work and personal obligations

Many struggle to preserve a work-life balance, but ADHD may make it more difficult. Those with ADHD may find it stressful to handle both job and personal life due to difficulty with executive function. A predisposition towards procrastination or perfectionism at work might further hinder your productivity if you feel you have too much on your plate.
You can worry about work during leisure, obsess about work, or feel terrible after work ends if the work-life balance isn't optimal.
Maintaining a regular schedule, creating routines around work, and avoiding overtime wherever feasible will assist if you need to enhance your work-life balance. The number of things you take on should be kept to a minimum.
While it may be difficult at first, you can eventually quit work at work to appreciate your guilt- and worry-free life.

Overconcentration on a single job

ADHD isn't only about being unable to concentrate; it's also about having trouble controlling your attention span.

Many persons with ADHD go through periods of hyperfocus, wherein they concentrate intensely on one subject. It describes a strong focus on one item that causes you to get engrossed and lose sight of time.

In certain circumstances, hyperfocus may increase productivity but can also cause distraction. If you often get engrossed in hyperfocus, it may be helpful to:

• Set a timer to help you monitor your time in hyperfocus.
• Set reminders for yourself to do other time-sensitive jobs before those that you could get too focused on.

Feeling overwhelmed and agitated

Even minor chores might feel daunting if you have ADHD. When you don't make much progress with your to-do lists because you are easily sidetracked and put them off, you could feel anxious, guilty, and even more, overwhelmed.

You put off work because you may need more time to accomplish it, yet you still think frequently about it. Even if you haven't scratched the surface of your to-do list, this might cause emotions of burnout and tiredness.

If you're overburdened, attempt to divide big jobs into easier-to-handle smaller ones. Maintaining a clean environment might assist since physical clutter can also be exhausting.

Being easily bored

While it's not a recognised sign of ADHD, being distracted easily and having trouble concentrating may lead to boredom.

Less fascinating tasks are less likely to keep your interest, which means you can become bored and wish to switch to something more exciting. It may include errands, jobs, or academic responsibilities.

Youngsters bored at school may lose interest in their studies, affecting their grades. Adults can become bored with some crucial professional activities or aspects of their relationships.

Even if you can't avoid certain jobs, you can make them more bearable by pausing and rewarding yourself when you finish. You may also change monotonous duties, like completing housework while listening to music.

3.6 Be Prepared To Find and Accept Help

Nobody should attempt to do tasks totally on their own. There is no shame in asking for assistance when and if you want assistance. Consult your primary care physician first. Ask them if they know anybody you should contact or if they recommend that you consult a mental health expert after explaining your particular issues or queries. You may discover solutions to increase your attention and reduce distractions with the assistance of an expert.

Social skills children with ADHD

Recognizing those close to you who are eager to assist is also crucial. Your loved ones want to help you but may not understand how. Informing others about your ADHD can help them better understand the symptoms and course of treatment, enhancing your interactions with them.

Requesting Social Support

Social support is essential for those living with ADHD. You pick who to share info with, but a great place to begin are with your spouse, friends, and close family members.
Next, you could alert your coworkers, managers, or instructors. When others around you understand what you're going through, they can assist you in overcoming the hurdles that ADHD might present at work or school. They could be more understanding whenever you request additional time for a certain assignment.

It might be difficult to comprehend how to discuss a disorder like ADHD when you get a diagnosis. Individuals might have a wide range of interpretations of what assistance entails, so it can be helpful to be clear about what you require from them.
Planning your talk is one of the finest methods to become at ease and confident throughout it.

Find relevant information on ADHD online and compile it for sharing. Based on everything you've studied, put together a phrase or two that describes ADHD using your own words. Consider potential questions other people might ask to prepare a solid response. It may also be helpful.

Other Resources

In addition to medicine and private counseling, joining a support group may help you manage your illness. It might relieve some of the stress on the family and friends to be able to communicate with others who have ADHD and understand what you're going through.

People with ADHD may exchange experiences, knowledge, and coping mechanisms in support groups, either online or in person. Local groups of ADHD organisations, social media, and websites of organisations are all places where you may discover support groups.

You can also think about getting in touch with a local social worker, a counsellor who specialises in helping individuals with ADHD, or a therapist who offers cognitive behavioural treatment for ADHD.

CHAPTER 4

ADHD and Other Possible Aggregate Conditions

4.1 Some Language Difficulties

The appropriate language acquisition throughout the child's development is crucial for the learning process, which may be negatively impacted by a language issue in ADHD that can manifest at any age and with varying degrees of severity. The irregularities in language are one of the most frequent comorbidities in ADHD. They lead to more unsatisfactory development, many issues with verbal and nonverbal skills, and even more issues in academic life due to losses in writing and reading appropriation.

For an effective evaluation of these patients both during and after the diagnosis process, it is crucial to understand the features of ADHD connected to the development, structure, and management of language in schools. To significantly contribute to speech treatment data confirming a new ailment without clear biomarkers.

The speech therapist then has the responsibility of intensively meddling in deficits which are outside the purview of the family or school but must be rectified by the specialist to achieve a more favourable and persistent school performance. It is performed to restrict mostly the results a treatment requires, which may entail the speech therapist.

4.2 Bipolar Behaviors

It makes sense that clinicians mistake ADHD symptoms for bipolar symptoms. These disorders are characterised by impulsivity, hyperactivity, irritability, emotional dysregulation, a racing mind, sleep issues, and difficulties with attentional control. Yet when you look closer, you can see how one state differs.
When BD is present, a doctor must do an ADHD evaluation on the patient. It is impossible to overstate how crippling and torturous this condition is, particularly for someone with ADHD. Given the high incidence of comorbidity, it is important to constantly check for the other when someone is identified with one.

Research of patients with BD and ADHD shows that they suffer from more mental illnesses than those with ADHD alone, as well as more acute ADHD symptoms and a younger age of beginning for BD. Patients having both ADHD plus BD are more likely to be male than those with BD alone, and the majority of them have behaviour problems or ODD diagnoses.
Remember that many trial participants were not promptly diagnosed and endured years of suffering. The prognosis may be changed with early diagnosis and therapy, which varies for each condition. A patient can lead a full, healthy life with the help of medicine, counseling, and life management.

4.3 Sleep management

A regular bedtime routine and good sleep hygiene habits may help reinforce the link between the bed and sleep for kids, teens, and adults with ADHD. Try adjusting and noting where you see benefits to create an effective system.
Some pointers are:

• Spending an hour preceding bed without using a screen
• Establishing a stress-free sleeping and sexual environment in the bed
• Establishing a nightly ritual that you like, such as having a warm bath, rereading a favourite book, or spending quality time with pets
• Establishing a regular bedtime and wake-up time and selecting a time that will allow you to achieve the required amount of sleep for the age group
• Eliminating alcohol, caffeine, and sweets a few hours before night
• Avoid engaging in stimulating activities and tasks that call for intense concentration in the evening
• Getting enough daytime sunshine and exercise

• Keeping the bedroom cold, dark, and quiet, and, if required, utilising a white noise generator to drown out distracting sounds
• Weighted blanket use

Often, people with ADHD say they have a hard time getting out of bed. Try light therapy or schedule a pleasant activity, like exercise or a delicious breakfast, once you start out of bed to assist you in getting off of the bed.

Adolescent children with ADHD who have trouble sleeping should be managed using a reward-based approach, according to the Adults and kids with ADHD organisation. In addition, parents may reassure their children by often checking on them. Every age group with ADHD may benefit from utilising relaxing strategies like guided imagery, chatting with a trusted advisor, or maintaining a worry diary. People with ADHD may not benefit from using sleep medications.
Still, some individuals may find it useful to speak with a doctor about taking additional vitamins or changing their prescription regimen to improve sleep. Some ADHD sufferers claim that taking their medicine approximately an hour after waking up increases daily attentiveness.

4.4 Obsessive-Compulsive Behaviors

Two mental health illnesses, ADHD and OCD, may have certain common symptoms. Yet because of its externalising character, ADHD impacts people's interactions with their surroundings. OCD, on the other hand, is internalising in nature, which means that when anxious, people tend to withdraw.
While there is a possible hereditary component to ADHD and OCD, the specific genetic basis of either disorder is unknown. Similar behavioural treatment and pharmaceutical regimens are used to treat both OCD and ADHD. The objectives of behavioural treatment and the kind of medicine that physicians recommend vary between the two, however. Because OCD and ADHD are treatable conditions, while people with both diseases often have more severe OCD symptoms, both disorders may be treated.

4.5 Depression

Those with ADHD are more likely to have suicide thoughts and behaviours in addition to depression. Suicidal thoughts are more likely to occur in young girls with ADHD and may be more likely in those with the hyperactive-impulsive subtype. Suicidal thoughts are a possible adverse reaction to several ADHD medicines. If you begin to have suicidal thoughts, you must immediately talk to your doctor.

Ask your kid with ADHD whether they have ever considered harming themselves, dying, or killing themselves if they seem sad. The sooner you learn, the quicker you can locate the finest and safest course of therapy.

Speak with your doctor as early as possible if you have been diagnosed with ADHD and believe you may also be depressed or if your kid has ADHD & you believe they may be depressed. These symptoms may be brought on by ADHD medication, which may be modified or adjusted.

It's also conceivable that depression is unrelated to the drug and requires further care. Don't hesitate to take notes while paying attention to your body, thoughts, and emotions. The hold of despair may be released, allowing you to lead an interesting and healthy life with the proper support and care.

4.6 Anxiety

Despite the possibility of co-occurring anxiety and ADHD, the latter is not the anxiety condition. Anxiety may sometimes happen without ADHD. Sometimes it might be brought on by having ADHD. When someone with ADHD forgets to prepare for a key test or misses a deadline at work, tension and worry might result. They may feel anxious even from neglecting to do such crucial responsibilities. These emotions and circumstances may result in an anxiety disorder if they persist, as they often do for persons with ADHD. Moreover, medicines had to treat ADHD, particularly stimulant drugs like amphetamines, may exacerbate anxiety symptoms. Genetics could also be important.

Strategies for managing stress and anxiety for children with ADHD

The combination of anxiety and ADHD may make ordinary tasks more challenging. Those with ADHD and anxiety may have much greater difficulty focusing on things. Hence, receiving appropriate care is crucial to ensuring a higher quality of life.

Since anxiety sometimes makes individuals scared to try new things, it may make treating ADHD more difficult. Moreover, new approaches may be required to manage ADHD to stay in front of the illness.

Treatment plans will change depending on the patient and the circumstance. The simultaneous treatment of both illnesses may be advantageous for some patients.

Sometimes, focusing on addressing only one of the problems may be more important. It could be acceptable if ADHD brings on anxiety since treating your ADHD can lessen the anxiety.

4.7 Hyperactivity

Hyperactivity is the term for excessive movements, such as fidgeting, high energy levels, moving about when seated, and chattiness. Decisions or acts performed on the spur of the moment are said to be impulsive.

Attention deficit hyperactivity disorder (ADHD)

If you're 17 years old or older, six or five of the following symptoms must regularly occur for a diagnosis of this kind of ADHD:

• Unable to remain sitting in a business or school
• Difficult to play or enjoy peaceful hobbies
• Talks excessively
• Has trouble waiting their turn, like while standing in line.
• Moves their hands, feet, or seat while fidgeting
• Runs around or climbs inappropriately
• Constantly moving, as though propelled by a motor
• Blurts out a response until a question is fully answered, for example, by finishing other people's sentences or speaking in the middle of a discussion.
• Disrupts or intrudes on others, for example, by joining in on games, activities, or discussions or by beginning to use other people's stuff without their consent. Adults and older adolescents may take up other people's tasks.

4.8 Provocative Behavior

ADHD is a diverse condition that often comes with low social skills and functioning. Since of their provocative, combative, or disruptive behaviour, 60% to 70%

of children with ADHD experience social rejection and stigma. These patients struggle to see and understand social signs, settle interpersonal disputes, and develop workable solutions.

From early pre-school years up to maturity, this affects their enjoyment and connections with classmates and teachers. Regarding its causes, several theories exist, ranging from dysfunctional involvement of brain regions involved in emotional and executive functioning to perceptual flaws in emotion recognition and failure in the sociocognitive abilities required to undertake competent social interaction. The key to treating ADHD's core symptoms and the social issues it causes or is related to is early diagnosis, pharmaceutical treatment, and psycho-educational intervention.

4.9 Aggressivity

When adults and children with ADHD become irrational and have anger management issues. It's crucial to provide your kid with the tools they need to cope with their emotions healthily if they often have outbursts of anger, particularly if these strong sentiments negatively impact their

education, relationships, and quality of life. There are methods you may use as an adult to deal with anger properly and prevent it from ruining your relationships and quality of life.

4.10 Defiant Behavior

Oppositional Defiant Disorder may be diagnosed when a child's recurrent misbehaviour interferes with their ability to function at school, at home, or with their classmates (ODD). The most frequent disease associated with ADHD is ODD. ODD often manifests before the age of eight. However, it may also affect teens. Among individuals they know well, like family members or even a regular care provider, children experiencing ODD may be more prone to become oppositional or rebellious.

These behaviours are more prevalent in children with ODD than in other kids their age.

ODD behaviours include, for instance:

• They often lose their cool
• Often feel wounded, resentful, or desire to harm someone they believe has wronged or given them issues.
• Often blaming others for their errors or bad conduct

- Disputes with adults or defiance of their wishes or rules
- Intentionally irritating others; quickly being irritated by people

4.11 Trouble Focusing

Children with inattentive ADHD have trouble focusing and adhering to directions. They often misplace items and forget things; they struggle to stay organised and finish tasks. The hyperactive-impulsive plus inattentive kinds of ADHD are combined in the majority of children.

Hyperactivity, inattention, and impulsivity are prominent signs of ADHD. Focusing poorly does not speak well of you and your work ethic.

Even though it may be difficult to maintain attention during tedious chores, there are techniques you may use to do so.

Keep in mind that not every strategy will be effective for you. The secret is to give it all a shot until you locate the one that works.

4.12 Restlessness

Adults with ADHD may:

- Struggle to remain still
- Move around often
- Shift in their position
- Tap their feet or hands

CHAPTER 5

Skills Necessary for Inclusion In Social Activities

5.1 The Development Of Conversational Skills

Language processing differs for kids with ADHD as well. They are more likely to have major linguistic deficits to start with. They are more prone to stray from the subject at hand while speaking due to their distractibility and associated ADHD symptoms, albeit without apparent delays. Also, they typically have trouble putting their ideas into coherent sentences and speaking fast. Even when the underlying abilities in this domain are strong, planning challenges may lead to grammatical mistakes when people construct sentences. Any ADHD-related symptoms, whether or not genuine language difficulties accompany them, may hinder successful communication.

Because of difficulties understanding quickly spoken language or distracting, loud surroundings like a party or a packed classroom, listening comprehension might be directly hampered by ADHD. It is true, once again, even if a kid doesn't have a language delay; while being able to comprehend, they overlook subtleties in both speech and tales due to ADHD.

They may overlook facts or lose track of discussion threads while listening, preventing them from registering important information. These similar gaps often come across as oppositional behaviour when a request seems to be purposefully

disregarded rather than just not being heard.
These tendencies are also connected to the reading comprehension issues often associated with ADHD.

In large gatherings or busy environments, paying attention to a topic of discussion might become even more difficult for a youngster with ADHD. Switching between speakers while maintaining attention on one speaker might not be easy. It has social repercussions since some ADHD youngsters have a simpler time getting along with people individually than in a group. Many activities occurring at once in a distracting classroom may make it extremely challenging for a youngster with ADHD to focus.

A youngster with ADHD often struggles to control lengthy speaking stretches simultaneously. Whereas another 8-year-old with strong comprehension may be able to withstand hearing up to twelve words at once, an ADHD patient may only manage seven or eight at a time. Any bigger information starts to fall out.
These difficulties in comprehending spoken language are sometimes misdiagnosed as an "auditory processing dysfunction." The information enters the auditory route normally; however, executive function deficits cause it to be mismanaged. Once again, your brain manager is dozing off while at work, confusing the specifics of what is being stated.

5.2 Problem-Solving

Problem-solving might become more challenging for people with ADHD when they have trouble recalling earlier events. Some individuals with ADHD could behave in an impulsive, unexpected way that they subsequently regret.
It has been theorized that ADHD is linked to issues with working memory maintenance and solving mathematical problems. Nevertheless, no research has been done on how updating affects children with ADHD's performance on arithmetic word problems.

A group of 11–12-year-old children with ADHD were compared to an identical control group of TDs with normal development to evaluate their performance while completing arithmetic word problems with low vs. high update requests. Findings indicated that children with ADHD made more mistakes while solving problems that required updating than when completing problems without updating requirements.
They also answered fewer problems properly than children who were normally developing. However, usually developing children did not exhibit any variations in their performance on challenges involving updated requirements. Analyses

of children's problem-solving techniques at a finer level revealed that children having ADHD found it more challenging than usually developing kids to identify the correct data before a calculation and to select and implement the right answer. The difficulty in choosing the right data worsens the issues with changing requirements.

Overall, these findings are consistent with the theory that the learning challenges experienced by children having ADHD are linked to executive dysfunctions that impair their ability to do complex tasks involving the updating of information still undergoing processing.

5.3 Conflict Resolution

In many relationships, it might be crucial to comprehend how ADHD and dispute resolution interact. Conflict will arise in every relationship, regardless of the person you are or the kind of your personality. All relationships may have conflicts from time to time, and if you don't know how to handle them effectively, the relationships will suffer as a whole.

The majority of individuals have trouble settling disputes. Part of this is a product of our self-centered society and individualism. Few of us desire to settle disputes since we believe we are always correct and don't need to.

Also, we put the onus of resolving any disconnect with the other people or parties. Yet the issue is never solved with this strategy. Instead, it often makes things considerably worse. Most individuals find that this method of conflict resolution works.

Conflict resolution slows for those with ADHD, but generally for different reasons. Sometimes, persons with ADHD find it difficult to identify or comprehend the feelings of others. They may not even know that conflict occurs due to their lack of empathy. Also, conflict resolution is even more challenging for those with ADHD who struggle to comprehend or articulate their feelings.

You must learn to control ADHD and handle conflicts to succeed in relationships.

5.4 Anger Control Conflict Resolution

After the day, you are on the first step in managing ADHD and resolving conflicts. Our natural reaction when problems emerge is to pick another person to share the blame and point the finger at. I reacted this way because they did that to me, or she said it. When a dispute arises, we portray ourselves as the victim and everybody else as the attacker.

We could be the one who is within the right or a victim of the dispute in some or perhaps many situations. Effective conflict resolution should still begin with your own emotions and how you handle conflict.

Nobody can be made to act in a certain manner by you. Rather, you may influence their behaviour by acting and reacting to others.

Respect for oneself and others are essential for effective conflict resolution. When allowing yourself to experience your emotions, it's important to acknowledge that many people have feelings and need a listening ear. It is why a big part of dispute resolution is listening to the other side and empathising with them.

It would help if you committed to improving yourself to start controlling ADHD and handling conflict better. When you find yourself in a fight, take a minute to evaluate how you are feeling, speak to others who are not involved in the conflict about how you are feeling, maintain your composure, make suggestions, and actively listen to discover answers. Even while it may not come naturally to you, you may become much better at conflict resolution with practise.

5.5 Anger Management

When children or adults having ADHD become irrational and have anger management issues, it's crucial to provide your kid with the tools they need to cope with their emotions healthily if they often have outbursts of anger, particularly if these strong sentiments negatively impact their education, relationships, and quality of life. There are methods you may use as an adult to deal with anger properly and prevent it from ruining your relationships and quality of life.

Find out what is causing your fury. Losing your temper easily over inconsequential things could indicate a more serious reason for your unhappiness. The little irritations could only serve as a momentary reason for your rage. Your health might be harmed by persistent rage. Limited evidence
suggests that hate and rage are related to heart disease, persistent discomfort,

trouble sleeping, and digestive issues.

Be mindful of anger's triggers and warning indications. You can tell when you're becoming furious physically because of your body. Here are a few red flags:

a racing heart, a headache, rapid breathing, clenching of the fists or jaw, or shoulder tension.

- Be calm and wait. Consider going for a run or a stroll.
- Talk it over.
- Employ "I feel" and other I-statements.
- Find techniques that help you relax.
- Visit a different activity.
- Discover more constructive methods to vent your rage.

My dear reader,

As the author of "Parenting Children with ADHD," I desire to remind you that at the heart of this book is the belief that every child deserves the chance to thrive and succeed, regardless of their challenges. And I know that as a parent, you share this belief.

This book is a labor of love, a culmination of years of research and personal experience. It is my hope that it will serve as a guiding light for parents who are navigating the complexities of ADHD.

But I cannot do this alone. I need your help. Your words have the power to inspire others to pick up this book and discover the transformative power of a strong and loving relationship with their child. Your review could make all the difference for another parent who is struggling to find their way.

So, my dear reader, I humbly ask that you take a moment to leave a review. Share your thoughts, your experiences, your hopes, and your dreams. Let us come together as a community, and support one another on this journey.

Thank you for your time, and for your commitment to raising happy, successful kids through strong and loving relationships.

Sincerely,

Grace S. Anderson

CHAPTER 6

Never Say This to Your Child

6.1 The 10 Common Phrases Not To Say

We all desire to reinstate some things we've said to our children while we were in a hurry because parents aren't flawless. Yet no matter how sore you get, there are several things you should never say to a kid with ADHD.

1. You're Dumber

Are you truly that foolish, lazy, or insane? Quit being so sluggish! You are competent in your field! How many times must I demonstrate? ... and so on. Everything that criticises them personally is stupid, stupid, or idiotic. I make an effort to prevent using the term "always." I do my best, but my son and I both realise that occasionally mom gets overwhelmed just like my kid does. We utilise my errors as teaching opportunities.

Many ADHD youngsters experience low self-esteem and guilt because they spend their schooldays trying to fit each round peg into the square hole. These suggestions can help your youngster feel more confident.

2. Why Are You Not Like Other?

Why are you unable to be like other children?
Never ask someone what's wrong with them.

You're not normal; never tell them. It isn't very good. I overheard that being uttered to a child, and it irritated me!

Most children with ADHD have social difficulties because they feel different from other schoolchildren and stick out badly. Please help your child develop the social skills necessary to establish friends with other children who will value his talents by teaching him that his differences make him fascinating.

3. If Just You'd Put Some Work into It...

I try not to use phrases like "If you'd just apply yourself" and "Just concentrate." With ADHD, it doesn't operate that way.

You aren't even trying.

You're so knowledgeable and brilliant; I was often complimented. Why won't you get the job done? I always said, "I don't know."

For kids and adults with ADHD, the focus is not a question of willpower. The chemistry of the brain regulates it. Less dopamine and other neurotransmitters, which regulate mood and attention, are produced by the ADHD brain. It won't alter by trying harder, although diet and exercise may help.

4. I wouldn't want anybody to have an ADHD child.

The phrase "I wouldn't want kids similar to you on anybody" is worse than "I hope you had kids exactly like yourself." It's traumatic to hear that. "

Never doubt your daughter's capacity to parent despite her ADHD. She will squander most of their life thinking that she "shouldn't" because she cannot handle it.

It's got, Justin Timberlake. The same applies to Karina Smirnoff, Lisa Ling, and Channing Tatum. In reality, many parents and very successful individuals have ADHD. Please share this with your kid and encourage him to aim high.

5. You're Exactly like Your Father.

Here, he gives suggestions for overcoming the guilt that often follows ADHD. Never remark, "If I had known he would obtain custody of you, I would never have married your father!" During the weekend, I just learned about this. It's vital to have a positive attitude towards the children throughout a divorce and refrain from disparaging the other parent in front of them.

Children with ADHD function best if their lives follow a regular, predictable pattern. Divorce may be very upsetting and worsen existing problems. Here are some suggestions for creating a timetable for each day, including weekends spent with Dad.

6. The Remarks That Hurt the Most

A lot of people speak insensitively. Myths and false information about ADHD are harmful. We know it's inappropriate when people blame all of us and our children for actions that the illness controls. Even the most devoted parents might sometimes be driven to speak in ways we later regret. Below, our readers listed a few phrases that should never be used to reprimand an ADHD youngster.

7. Never use "but," always say, "I love you, Plus I can't allow you..." or "You made a horrible decision, But I love you much to..."

I constantly wait before the word "but" because I am aware that the moment I say it, he will take all of the criticism to heart. The excellent and useful alternative is "AND"!

One drop or two of little praise is like rain in the desert for a youngster with ADHD. Dr Ned Hallowell says he takes it all in and enjoys it. Following are his suggestions for improving the use of positive reinforcement.

8. You Didn't Take Your Medicine Today.

You won't give your medication today, did you? is a phrase everyone in my home, including myself, has become used to uttering. Or "We ought to have given you your medication today," etc. We've constantly tried to stop everyone from doing it since it severely offends his sentiments.

While brain chemistry is the cause of ADHD symptoms, your kid does not have to feel helpless in the face of them. Inform her about the neurological and physical advantages of a high-protein, frequent exercise, low-sugar diet, and appropriate vitamins and supplements for ADHD sufferers.

9. You Should Feel Guilty.

I was often told, "You ought to be ashamed of yourself," growing up. I felt terrible about myself as a result. I still struggle with low self-esteem and lack of confidence like an adult with ADHD. Overcoming such outdated messages is challenging. By the age of 10, people who have ADHD are thought to have received 20,000 more negative signals than good ones. According to ADHD specialist Dr Ned Hallowell, these people see themselves as essentially wrong and different.

10. I Detest You.

In a rage, my buddy, who has an ADHD kid, said, "I hate you." For people on the outside, it may be quite difficult to comprehend how irritating ADHD can be. It's

crucial to comprehend that children cannot regulate their conduct."
I respond to my child's "I detest you" by saying, "You ain't no peach either." Just go to your room and consider the cause of your rage; when you're ready, speak to me. That sometimes works, and I get an apology.

6.2 The 10 Common Negative Behaviors

Defiant and violent conduct is the most frequent issue among children with ADHD. It involves disobeying parenting or academic instructions (more frequently than other youngsters). Children may have emotional outbursts when asked to accomplish difficult or demanding activities.

According to Dr Vasco Lopes, an expert in ADHD with disruptive behaviours, children with ADHD tend to become stubborn in certain circumstances.

These circumstances include being asked to do tasks like schoolwork, go to sleep, put a game down, take a seat, and eat meals. Due to the deficiencies associated with ADHD, they struggle to endure these settings.

They consist of the following:

1. Often becoming enraged or losing control
2. Keeping an eye out
3. Disagreeing with adults or disobeying their norms or demands
4. Accepting a dull circumstance
5. Often bitter or hateful
6. Limiting impulsivity
7. The intentional annoyance of others or irritation of others
8. Leaving an enjoyable activity
9. Blaming for one's errors or bad conduct on others
10. Limiting their amount of exercise

Kids may fight, behave aggressively, or appear angry or stubborn with adults. A behaviour disorder may be identified when these annoying behaviours are unusual for the child's age, continue over a moment, or are severe. Disruptive conduct disorders are called externalising disorders since they include acting out and displaying inappropriate behaviour towards others.

CHAPTER 7

ADHD at School

7.1 How Educators Can Help Children with ADHD

Teachers and educators have a special opportunity to support kids and teenagers in realising their academic potential. Most educators are seeking more information about ADHD and ways to enhance the learning environment for their pupils.

Education of children with ADHD

Children experiencing attention-deficit/hyperactivity disorder (ADHD) have greater challenges than the typical student in achieving success.
Children having this diagnosis may find it challenging to do well in school because of the symptoms of ADHD, which include difficulties paying attention, difficulty being still, and problems managing impulses.

Schools may provide services to help kids with ADHD achieve their needs.

• ADHD therapies include organisational training or behavioural classroom management
• Accommodations to decrease the impact of ADHD on students learning
• Special education assistance

7.2 Why Collaborate With Teachers

It is crucial for kids with ADHD to have instructors who are aware of how the disorder affects their academic performance. The better instructors are at assisting their pupils, the more effective methods they are aware of. There has never been a greater pressing need for teaching strategies tailored specifically for ADHD students to help them perform better and succeed in school.
Let's explore e advice that will assist you and the teacher in having the most fruitful connection possible now that you know

Discuss the best times and methods to communicate. Ensure you keep things simple for a teacher if they spend additional time working with you. You may ensure that they won't feel overloaded by choosing the most effective channels and times for communication with them.

Don't personalise situations. You could sometimes hear something from your child's instructor that you don't agree with. Hearing that your kid speaks too much or has trouble making friends may be difficult. Recognize that you plus the instructor belong to the same team and that they are just providing you with information to assist you.

Together, try out new things. There may be occasions when the instructor or you come upon a novel technique. Don't let it prevent you from giving it a go. Only one method determines if it will or won't work.

Get in touch often. While the school may plan parent-teacher conferences regularly, you should speak to the teacher more often. You can learn about any critical knowledge much more quickly if you do this.

Inform your family of any changes that might affect your academics. Your child's behaviour at school may be impacted by anything at home. For instance, it might be beneficial for teachers to know if their kid substantially depends on a schedule that will be disturbed for a few weeks due to a family visit in instance they start to notice how it affects them at school.

Be receptive to the teacher's advice. Be prepared to allow them to succeed if the instructor advises your kid to attempt a new routine or other test-taking techniques. These might result in some major advancement.

7.3 When to Let Teachers Do It

Low grades, reprimands and punishment, bullying from classmates, and poor self-esteem are common consequences of ADHD in kids and teenagers. As a result, you, the teacher, end up fielding inquiries from parents who believe their children are being ignored in the classroom because you cannot reach a child with ADHD. Nevertheless, things don't have to turn out this way. There are methods you may take to assist children with ADHD in overcoming their learning difficulties, maintaining their attention without bothering others, and doing well in the classroom.

7.4 Practical Tips and Tricks to Help Him Learn

Attention is affected in people with ADHD due to changes in their brains. Compared to those without it, they are more susceptible to distraction. They often struggle with remaining organised, maintaining attention, and completing tasks. ADHD also has an impact on behaviour. Some individuals can struggle to remain quiet, wait, or pay attention. Some people make too many interruptions or irritate easily. Some people hurry through tasks rather than taking their time. ADHD impacts several individuals in various ways.

If you suffer from ADHD, you know how frustrating and misunderstood it may sometimes seem.

Doing your best at home, work, and with friends is more difficult when you have ADHD. You don't have to let that stop you, however. Learn everything you can instead of this.

There is no easy remedy; managing ADHD requires patience. Taking medication or seeing a therapist are two options for managing ADHD. Most ADHD sufferers engage in both.

Try these more suggestions to assist with schoolwork:

While completing your schoolwork, turn off your phone. It also reduces interruptions.

Use tools that can keep you organised. Use a phone app or a calendar to keep track of your assignments. Make a list of what you must carry home. To remember lessons and events, set a phone reminder or write them down in a planner.

Take pauses for exercise. Ask your professors if you may take short pauses throughout the class to stand up and walk about if you're feeling antsy. As you go back to your seat and do this, it might help you regain concentration. Take frequent pauses from studying or doing your schoolwork.

Consider all the positive aspects of yourself. One aspect of you is ADHD. There is a tonne more, too. Think about things people enjoy about you. You could be witty, kind, or creative. Maybe you are gifted in music, dancing, athletics, or the arts. You could be skilled in technology, construction, or cuisine. Give your favourite activities some time. Use your strengths every day to develop them. You spend time with those who accept you for the person you are. That's how you see yourself, too.

To reduce distractions, **sit at the front of the class.**

Discuss your ADHD with your instructor. Some ADHD children need more testing time. Some students want smaller classes or a quiet area to do their work. Others require a tutor. It would help if you enlisted your teacher's assistance in planning and self-care.

Take a lot of walks. For persons with ADHD, regular exercise may enhance their attention span and academic performance. Also, it keeps your good feelings going.

Take up meditation. Mindfulness Meditation may enhance concentration, memory, and attention. It may also lessen tension. It is simple to learn. Please spend a few minutes doing it each day.

7.5 Study Techniques

You may not know where to start when it comes to studying if you or your kid has ADHD.

Several tried-and-true strategies and study techniques are effective for persons with ADHD, regardless of age or grade. By doing them often, you may develop positive habits that will enhance your grades and reduce your overall stress.

Before we go through our top ten study suggestions, we want to emphasise the importance of getting enough sleep, particularly if you suffer from ADHD.

Learning strategies for children with ADHD

According to research, a person having ADHD has a tougher time remembering things the more sleep issues they have.

Therefore, try to get a decent night's sleep every night, particularly before a major exam.

Therefore, these suggestions won't make a late-night study session less crucial.

Study advice for ADHD sufferers

Here are a few strategies that work well for managing issues at school for persons with ADHD.

1. Check your thoughts

Next, check your thoughts. It means assessing your emotional state. Are you joyful, sad, enraged, or mad? Address any powerful emotions you may be experiencing.

It would help to write down your feelings or talk to a parent or tutor. Before you begin studying, you must express everything in your thoughts. The issue cannot be solved right now. Said it's time to let it out.

Once you've stated your thoughts, think about engaging in some deep breathing techniques for a few minutes to let the remainder of your stress out.

Your mind-body assessment will likely take ten minutes or so.

2. Organize yourself

Plan. Start by looking at everything you need to accomplish and ensuring you have everything.

Take a sheet of paper and create a chart containing three columns as follows:

I. Include your to-do list in the first column.

II. Estimate the length of time it will require you to complete it in the second column. Try giving yourself extra time for each work you may need.

III. For the time being, leave its third column empty; it will be used to indicate how long it takes.

Afterwards, arrange your tasks in the order you wish to do them, assigning numbers to each.

3. Read your work again

People with ADHD often jump right in. Yet, you must be aware of what is required of you, including what you must know and write.

Then, you may choose how to meet them after you are familiar with the job requirements.

Before you begin, note all your requirements, such as the number of pages, word count, necessary references, etc.

While you work on the project, you may go to this list and mark each item off as you finish it.

4. Recognize your own needs and what might work for you

Finding your preferred method of operation may be a process since everyone works differently. Consider making notes on your successes and failures.

You may find it useful to ask yourself things like:

• Can exercise aid improve concentration?
• Can saving stuff till the last help you learn more?
• Can you concentrate better in the evening or after dinner?
• Do you do better work if you start right away when you come home from school?
• Do you require a brief rest period of 30 minutes before starting?
• Do you, for instance, struggle to begin an essay?
• Do your smartphone or other displays tend to draw your attention? If so, think about taking them off while you study.
• How have you previously overcome writer's block?
• Must it be something you're interested in for you to be able to hyperfocus on it?
• Would you like to overcome your greatest fear following a straightforward victory? Doing the simplest activity first to feel better about it, and then taking on the one you hate helps?

Many people do! While it might be challenging, no law says you should write your introduction first.

Indeed, many individuals write their introduction & conclusion after finishing the essay's body.

Hence, if writing the supporting paragraphs first and then the introduction is simpler for you, go for it.

It could be simpler to begin by writing freely and without any expectations. What comes out could surprise you.

5. Make the requisite arrangements

Any techniques your educators or school utilise to meet your needs are considered accommodations in this context, such as placing you in a separate suite for an exam or giving you more time.

For instance, if you're experiencing trouble recollecting math formulas, you might ask your teacher to give them to you during the test.

Accommodations level the playing field rather than providing you with an edge. Tests should gauge your aptitude rather than any limitations.

If you don't have such accommodations, all you are testing is your handicap.

6. Start a body scan

Conduct a body scan when you've located your position. Check every part of your body to see whether you are indeed hungry. Do I need water? Do I have to go to the restroom? What will I need for the body?

You cannot learn effectively if your body is not well-nourished and comfortable.

7. Be truthful about your fears

Whether you're doing homework, writing a project, or prepping for an exam, one aspect of the job ahead appears the most frightening.

What's the best method to approach that? Declare it aloud.

What scares you the most right now? Are you worried you will never complete that lengthy assignment since you're so far behind? Are you concerned that you won't succeed because you don't comprehend the subject? Please put it in writing.

You're not starting because of that dread. Nevertheless, once you've said or written it down, you're no longer constrained by your fear and can continue.

8. Begin with a little assignment

If you're having trouble getting started, you should succeed immediately since it will inspire you. Then start your study session by working on any little assignment.

Get started when you've learned about the task or exam.
Those with ADHD could have a propensity towards procrastination. Yet begin-

ning sooner may alleviate much tension and boost your scores overall.

Studies show that although studying for an exam might help you retain material temporarily, you'll rapidly forget it.

You'll be better able to recall the material if you study over time. It is crucial in math and physics because your knowledge expands on your prior knowledge.

Working backwards is advised. Consider the date of your exam or the deadline for your task, and make a strategy to do a bit each day. Be sure to provide time for writing and editing your assignment or reviewing everything before a test.

9. Repeating yourself endlessly

Repetition is crucial since studying is all about performance. Many individuals with ADHD may struggle with working memory, making remembering new information difficult. Hence, read the material repeatedly, take notes during class, and review everything often.

A three-times rule is good. You review each section at least three times, especially if it is a topic you know about.

10. Give yourself a treat

Jot down how it required you to complete each item on your to-do list, then treat yourself.

The instant reward may be whatever you want, a little dance party, a block stroll, or messaging a buddy. Nonetheless, it should only last a few minutes.

7.6 Plan and Organize Lean

Becoming organised is often challenging for people with ADHD. Yet, you may learn to become organised with a few adjustments and trial and error. Check out these suggestions to determine what suits your needs and way of life the best.

I study and work with ADHD:

Don't use paper
Monthly statements, invoices, and bills don't necessarily have to be sent to you. Electing to receive them online might help you eliminate paperwork around your house.

Make decision bags
Being unsure might slow down the organising process.

Write lists
Lists are excellent tools for organisations. They can assist you in establishing a beginning point and identify all that must be done.

Mark off accomplishments
A sensation of forward motion and success may be generated by crossing off tasks as you do them.

Use coloured pens or markers
The colour you choose for your labels may remind you of critical chores and an alarm to urgency.
According to research, colours like yellow and red are easier to recall than blue and green.

Save all important papers in one location
Building a different stack for every essential document type might be tempting. But you may save time and space by keeping your crucial documents in one location.

Use transparent trash cans
Instead of taking down each storage container to see inside, clear bins can let you rapidly scan for the items you need.

Speak about your activities
Speaking aloud about a job you're attempting to do might help you concentrate. It could also let other family members know you might need assistance remaining on track.

Each day, concentrate on one thing
You can complete chores by breaking them down and keep up with this practice every week.
You may develop organisational habits and build a pattern by allocating work to certain days.
For example, you may fold clothes on Monday and ask for your bank statements on Tuesday.

Utilize images
You can sometimes understand a picture with more than one word. Images may be used to substitute labels or constantly remind us of objectives.
Plan to spend more time
Allowing oneself more time for tasks, occasions, or appointments helps relieve deadline anxiety.

Establish modest objectives
You may feel more successful if you divide difficult tasks into smaller ones. Some jobs could seem more manageable if they are broken down even more.

Put time management first
Since time management and organisation are closely connected skills, you may strengthen one by strengthening the other.

Place a garbage or recycle container in each room
You may dispose of papers or goods faster by placing a trash can and a recycling bin in each room rather than accumulating them for later disposal.

Arrange as soon as possible
You may avoid spending hours now at the end of the week putting things in order by organising consistently throughout the day.

Be surrounded by encouraging individuals
When we feel like damaged goods, it is challenging to function in the neurotypical environment. Be in the company of individuals who respect you and your quick thinking.

Make sure everything has its place
You could find things easier to discover and store quickly if you give them a home. Put up bins and storage containers where goods may be put or kept. A box for irrelevant mail that may be recycled and another containing bills and stuff to attend to.

Simplify
Fewer objects must be stored or managed when superfluous or unwanted goods are removed from the house.

Make use of visual cues
You may find it easier to keep on target if you colour-code your stuff. You may choose a colour to stand for every day of the week or designate a colour to indicate quick attention.
Using object orientation to assist with staying organised could also be beneficial. Turning the shampoo bottle upside down when you run out of shampoo, for instance, may allow you to recall to obtain a new one.

Get specific
Lists are useful tools, but you could benefit more by including extra information.

Create two separate lists, one for today and the other for tomorrow, with at least 2 urgent and two essential tasks on each list for each day.

Label each item
You may put things away more quickly and spend less time hunting for things you need by labelling the storage containers or bins you use for organising.

Convenience is key
A significant component of an organisation might be positioning oneself for success. Putting objects near wherever you use them might make them simpler to set aside or manage if you require them.
For instance, having your hamper in the laundry room might make grabbing soiled items on wash day simple.

Give vital things a pass
Dr Quinn notes that persons with ADHD may find it more difficult to complete chores like keeping track of a chequebook and paying payments.
Separate ensembles, not items of clothing
Keep your clothes things together if you have ensembles you often wear to save time. You may expedite your morning preparations by putting your clothes away the night before.

Maintain a paper calendar
Posting a sheet or whiteboard calendar for everyone to see as a daily visual reminder of future tasks might be helpful.

Employ technology-based alerts
An electronic calendar can help you organise your schedule and remain on task.

Remember to check your glove box
Disarray may sometimes be seen within the automobile. Your glovebox should only include the insurance cards, current registration, owner's handbook, and a flashlight.

Keep storage areas compact
A lack of structure may result from having too much of something. Keeping storage spaces compact may restrict how much you may keep.

Make notes for yourself
Sticky notes may remind you of things you need to accomplish and things you've put off.
You may find it helpful to return to a task later if you leave a note outlining whe-

rever you are.

To say "no," practise
Even though it may not be simple, declining a request for a favour might help you avoid overscheduling your day.

7.7 Homework, the Best Workout

For kids who have ADHD, homework may be extremely frustrating and challenging. By setting up a neat and relaxing study area in your house, you may, as a parent, assist your kid in feeling less frustrated. It may be a desk, a kitchen table, or a floor mat. The ideal location has few distractions but allows your kid to be close to you or another adult.

Your kid might develop the habit of doing their homework every time people sit down to complete it if they have a specific area for it. Your youngster learns how to plan and arrange their time and ideas while also starting to equate that area with becoming productive and focused.

7.8 Public speaking Approach

Now that we are aware of all the limitations and challenges that ADHD may bring, it is obvious to us that possessing it can greatly influence the ability to speak in public. Despite the challenges of having ADHD, there are steps you may take to improve your public speaking abilities.

Prepare your speech
Before writing your speech, create a mental map or overview of what you'd like to say and the best way to express it. It might help you find the areas where your presentation needs improvement. It's also a great chance to ask your tutor, parent, teacher, or neighbourhood library for assistance.
It would help if you remembered that a simple theme is preferable to a complicated one. Your viewers will get disinterested if your framework is extremely complex. No matter how fascinating your subject is, try to stay away from being too complicated.

Prepare yourself
Creating cue cards for your speech before giving it in public is always a smart idea. A diagnosis of ADHD or not, it's risky to memorise your speech exactly. Create cue cards with all the pertinent information so you won't forget anything. Your cue cards should be bright, too. Likewise, true for underlining the texts; this

could help reinforce their significance in your thoughts.

If you commit your speech to memory phrase by phrase, there is a good possibility that if you miss a few crucial phrases, you will forget the whole speech. Moreover, it is commonly known that people with ADHD struggle with memory and often forget things. While you should get comfortable with your speech, avoid copying it literally.

Maintain consistent eye contact

Although you can't truly practise with a real audience, you can practise with stuffed animals on the bed if you're a young child. Imagine them to be the actual people who will be listening to you talk in public as you position them right in front of you.

To prepare for the speech day, maintain consistent eye contact. Practice keeping eye contact after lifting your head from the script if you want to hold your notes.

Focus on Success

The night before your speech, see yourself delivering an impactful speech instead of failing to do so. Imagine giving a presentation in a classroom in which everyone is listening and you are making frequent eye contact. Suppose all of your preparations were successful.

Being a competent public speaker requires you to have self-confidence.

Choose a fascinating subject

Those with ADHD are more inclined to hold on to their feelings. Think of it as an advantage rather than a drawback! Choose a subject that appeals to you and will enable you to give a moving speech. Your passion will permeate across the crowd if you do this. Try to think of a unique way to tackle a dry topic if it has been given to you. Search for alternate methods or concepts or freshly reframe things.

Rewrite

Remember that your objective is to make your speech or presentation brief and to the point while presenting it. If you only repeat your thoughts, the audience may find you dull if you have ADHD and is prone to tossing all the ideas simultaneously. Always focus on the important topics to prevent this.

When you complete the first draught, think about revising your talk at least twice. Always bear in mind that keeping things short is the main objective. Also, you should highlight your important points, organise the information better, use more appropriate language, etc. Your presenting abilities may be considerably enhanced by doing this.

A recording of you

Any device may be used to record oneself speaking. Watch the videos once they've been recorded, then add comments about what you enjoy and don't enjoy about them.

It is among the best techniques for finding errors that need to be fixed and great qualities that need to be kept. It would help if you considered how to make the speech more interesting. The speech's opening and ending need extra attention. Your actions also count for something in addition to what you say.

You may accustom your speech with this method and learn where your weaknesses are. If you view the recorded video numerous times, you'll remember this!

Develop your timing

Timing is crucial in a presentation while speaking in front of an audience. You will therefore comprehend why presenters must adhere to their allowed time.

Individuals with ADHD tend to talk quicker than usual, which makes them regularly fall well short of the permitted time and makes their speech seem useless. They usually go from silence to lightning-quick because they are anxious and want to get off the platform as soon as possible.

You'll need a little digital timer or stopwatch on your phone to practise. It would help if you talked swiftly enough to prevent rambling while speaking slowly to be understood. It is important to manage your time well.

7.9 When Schools Resist Evaluating and Addressing ADHDs

As per the Centers for Disease Control and Prevention, almost two-thirds of kids with ADHD have at least one other illness; learning issues impact 46% of them, anxiety disorders 32% of them, mood disorders 17% of them, and autistic spectrum disorders 14% of them.

Yet, despite the commonality of co-occurring disorders, activists, psychologists, and learning specialists, say that many ADHD adolescents do not initially obtain a testing for common comorbidities.

CHAPTER 8

Proper Nutrition

8.1 Ease the Symptoms with the Proper Diet

For kids with ADHD, eating vegetables and fruits is a smart idea since it may assist with inattention problems, according to recent research.

Including vegetables and fruits in a balanced diet may help to lessen certain symptoms of ADHD.

Children who received the micronutrients are three times more likely to significantly improve their symptoms of ADHD and behavioural dysregulation compared to those who received a placebo, according to the research that examined the supplement's efficacy.

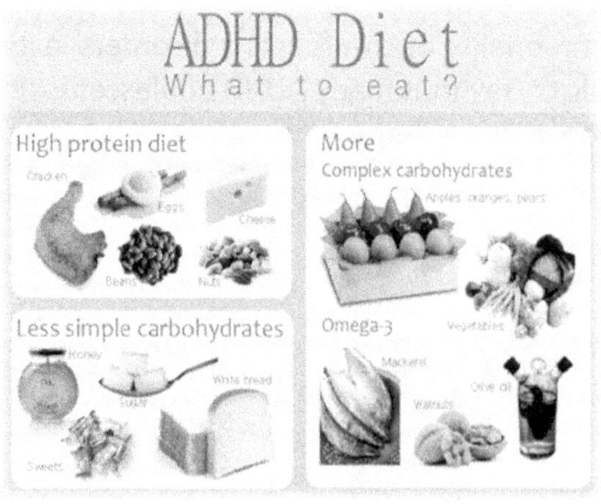

A balanced diet that includes all nutrients kids need may aid in easing their ADHD symptoms.
As children having ADHD begin exhibiting excess symptoms, physicians often raise the dosage of the medicinal treatment while they're taking one or start them on it. Our research indicates the importance of examining the children's nutrition and availability of food to determine whether either factor may increase the intensity of their symptoms.
Two weeks before the study started, participants were drug-free or had quit using their prescribed medications.
Based on information gathered when the kids initially signed up for the trial, before they started taking a micronutrient placebo or supplement, the studies on fruit and vegetable consumption and the impact of food poverty.

Why may nutrition play such a big role in ADHD?
Fewer levels of certain neurotransmitters within the brain are thought to be a contributing cause of ADHD, and minerals and vitamins are essential cofactors in the body's production of these critical neurochemicals and normal brain function.

Food insecurity could also be a factor.
Children having ADHD are no different from everyone else when it comes to being frustrated when they are hungry. Their symptoms can worsen if they aren't eating enough.
Moreover, family conflict may exacerbate ADHD symptoms in children by the stress from parents concerned that they will be unable to feed their kids enough.

It is crucial since Western meals are more prone to be short in vegetable and fruit consumption than others, including the Mediterranean diet.

Before establishing or altering a treatment plan, doctors, in our opinion, should evaluate the level of food security felt by kids with ADHD.

By assisting families in providing a healthy diet and increasing their food security, certain symptoms may be easier to control.

8.2 Best Proteins

Diets high in protein aid in enhancing mood, regulating ADHD symptoms, and lowering the chance of developing depression. It was shown as children having ADHD who had a high-protein diet performed better cognitively compared to those who did not. It has been shown that high-protein diets are useful in treating ADHD. It is due to the ability of high protein diets to lower hormone levels related to stress and enhance cognition, which results in improved attention and decreased disruptive behaviours. Little evidence supports the association between gluten, nightshades, dairy, wheat, and ADHD.

The brain produces various chemical messengers called neurotransmitters to control alertness and sleep. Neurotransmitters that cause alertness are released by protein, while carbs bring on sleepiness.

These results confirm the widespread perception that having breakfast and lunch high in protein helps persons with ADHD function better. A protein-rich breakfast increases alertness and lessens the risk that ADHD medication may result in irritation or restlessness.
Proteins influence brain function by supplying the amino acids needed to make neurotransmitters. Biochemical messengers called neurotransmitters to send messages from one brain cell to the other. Your ADHD kid will be more awake in class, or you will be more organised at work due to the quality of the food you provide these messengers.

Tryptophan and tyrosine, two amino acids, are crucial components of neurotransmitters. These amino acids impact the production of the top four neurotransmitters, tryptophan-derived serotonin and tyrosine-derived dopamine, adrenaline, and norepinephrine. One vital amino acid is tryptophan. The body cannot produce it; it must come from food. If there is low tyrosine in the diet, the body can produce it.

Start your day with a protein-rich breakfast since protein helps your body produce brain-awakening neurotransmitters.
Protein helps maintain stable blood sugar levels and protects against the mental deterioration that results from consuming an excessive amount of simple carbohydrates.
Don't be alarmed if sugary cereals, bread, or doughnuts are your family's preferred breakfast options. You don't have to consume a plate of bacon and eggs every morning for your daily protein needs.
Depending on age, children require between 24 and 30 grammes of protein daily. People require between 45 and 70 grammes. One cup of milk but rather soy milk, an egg, or one ounce of meat or cheese all contain 7 grammes.

8.3 Beware of this: Sugar

Although it's doubtful that sugar substantially impacts ADHD symptoms directly, proper eating habits are crucial for everyone, including those with ADHD. It involves using sugar sparingly.

Blood sugar spikes, such as those brought on by consuming sugary meals or highly processed starches and grains, and the subsequent blood sugar falls may affect mood, impair concentration and attention, and produce energy fluctuations in those with and without ADHD.

Among the methods to reduce the effect and consumption of sugar are:

• Keep the treats until later, when concentration is less crucial.
• When you desire something sweet, go for fruit. Fruit still includes sugar but has fibre to prevent a blood sugar surge and healthful minerals.
• While eating meals or snacks, particularly those that include sugar or processed carbs, ensure you have a protein source.
• Eat often to reduce blood sugar swings and your propensity to seek something sweet.
• If you consume a lot more sugar, taper your consumption by gradually replacing the sweets you are reducing with more nutritious items.

8.4 Omega 3s: Fill the Bag

Omega-3 fatty acids are important for treating and preventing ADHD.

Having ADHD is more likely if you consume fewer omega-3 fatty acids. Those who consumed a diet deficient in omega-3s showed a 31 per cent greater chance of being identified with ADHD, according to a study of almost 200 pupils.

Blood levels for omega-3 fatty acids are lower in children with ADHD diagnoses. Children with ADHD often have blood levels for omega-3 fatty acids that are 38% lower than those without the illness. In research involving 493 kids, individuals having lower blood levels for DHA displayed higher levels of anger, disobedience, mood swings, and academic problems. Also, a study by UK researchers found that children having ADHD and low omega-3 levels exhibited impaired emotion management, as well as poor emotion understanding and processing.

Children experiencing ADHD may have low omega-3 levels genetically. Keep in mind that ADHD does not represent a behavioural issue. It is a medical condition that causes low dopamine, serotonin, and norepinephrine levels and typically has a hereditary component. They looked at 180 children having ADHD versus 180 children without the condition. They discovered that ADHD children were 60–70% more likely to have a mutation in a gene required for fatty acid metabolization.

Irregular brain waves and low omega-3 levels. According to research published in the journal Neuropharmacology, ADHD youngsters with low blood levels of

DHA exhibit a particular sort of chaotic brain activity connected to ADHD.

8.5 Iron and other Fundamentals Minerals

The severity of the symptoms increases with the quantity of ferritin, the protein found within cells that stores iron. A little research found that iron supplements helped children with ADHD who were iron deficient in their symptoms.
Certain dietary supplements may support ADHD medications and aid in relieving symptoms that impact focus, mood, memory, and cognitive function. These supplements could include proteins, lipids, vitamins, and minerals.
The natural ADHD supplements mentioned below include components often used for ADHD but have studies to support their claims.

But, bear in mind that further studies are required to discover if supplements for ADHD are useful.
Children with low blood ferritin levels responded well to iron supplementation of 80 mg daily, indicating the need for further research,
including bigger controlled trials. The efficiency of iron treatment is equivalent to that of stimulants, and it was well tolerated.

8.6 Why is Natural better?

Treatments without a doctor's prescription are known as natural cures for ADHD plus other illnesses. People have used natural treatments to solve their health problems for thousands of years. These treatments, now more typically referred to as complementary & alternative medicine (CAM), sometimes entail dietary modifications, supplements, and lifestyle adjustments.
Although complementary and alternative therapies may potentially be effective in treating ADHD, medication may still be required to address the condition. The best method for treating and controlling symptoms may be a mix of treatments.
Natural treatments for ADHD may be used in place of or in addition to medications recommended by a doctor. But before attempting an alternative therapy, always speak with a healthcare professional.

8.7 More recurring food sensitivities in ADHD

Food sensitivity is obvious when a meal triggers a person's physical or behavioural symptoms, but testing doesn't reveal a real allergy. Stomachaches, headaches, rashes, or, throughout the situation of ADHD, increased impulsivity, hyperactivity, and lack of attention may all be symptoms of food sensitivity. A kid may still be sensitive to particular foods even when a skin or blood test regarding food allergies comes back negative.

Although any meal may be troublesome, studies have indicated that the following foods are most often linked to symptoms of ADHD:

- Dairy products
- Corn
- Oats
- Nuts and peanuts
- Chocolate
- Yeast
- Shellfish
- Gluten
- Soy
- Legumes
- Eggs
- Citrus
- Tomato
- Fish

8.8 Food Intolerances and Allergies

It's critical to differentiate between food allergies and food sensitivities. A blood or skin test may diagnose a food allergy, an allergic response to a specific food. While some may, the majority of children experiencing ADHD lack food sensitivities.

8.9 Dietary Supplements: Do They Help?

Although useful, ADHD-friendly vitamins may not have the same quick and potent impact on ADHD symptoms as medication. Comparing the efficacy of these supplements to medicine is challenging. On average, supplements have significantly fewer adverse effects than medications and are less likely to have serious negative effects. As a component of an integrated therapy strategy that also includes treatments for education, parenting, sleep, and exercise, we utilise supplements.

8.10 Drinks with Caffeine and High Concentration of Glucose, Soda: Effects on ADHD

Some persons with ADHD may benefit from small quantities of coffee. According to some studies, it may improve focus. Caffeine, however, may amplify the effects of several ADHD drugs, including any negative side effects which a person may encounter.
Caffeine consumption should be restricted for adults with ADHD, particularly if they use ADHD medicines. Kids or teens should never consume coffee, tea, and cola.

Blood glucose spikes and crashes may be brought on by sugary meals, which can impact energy levels. Some parents claim that children with ADHD who consume sugar are more hyperactive. Although some study suggests a correlation between high sugar plus soft drink intake and a greater rate of ADHD diagnoses, other research shows no such association. Limiting sugar consumption is a healthy decision for everyone, even if it does not help ADHD symptoms, since it may lower the risk of obesity, diabetes, and tooth decay.

CHAPTER 9

Good Practices and Experience in ADHD Treatment

9.1 Natural Remedies for ADHD

Alternative, more natural choices are available if you feel uncomfortable treating this disease with medication.

Management of attention and hyperactivity in children with ADHD

1. Steer clear of allergies
Some ADHD children's behaviour may be improved by diets that limit potential allergens.
If you think your kid may have allergies, seeing a specialist specialising in allergies is advisable. But you may try it out by avoiding these things:

• Eggs and milk
• Processed food products, including potato chips, dry cake mixes, chewing gum, cereal, instant mashed potatoes, and butter, commonly include chemical additives/preservatives like BHT (butylated hydroxytoluene) & BHA (butylated hydroxyanisole) that are employed to prevent the oil in a product from going bad.
• Salicylates are compounds that occur naturally in plants and are present in various foods, including berries, apples and cider, chilli powder, grapes, peaches,

oranges, prunes, plums, and tomatoes. They are also a key component of many painkillers: Chocolate.

2. Attend a yoga / tai chi session.

According to a few tiny studies, yoga may be beneficial as an additional treatment for ADHD sufferers. Boys with ADHD who frequently practised yoga while taking their regular meds showed substantial improvements in anxiety, hyperactivity, and social issues.

Tai chi may potentially assist in reducing ADHD symptoms. Researchers discovered that tai chi exercise reduced anxiety and hyperactivity in adolescents with ADHD. When they attended tai chi courses twice a week for five weeks, they also daydreamed less and showed fewer inappropriate emotions.

3. Parenting or behavioural treatment

Behavioural treatment may be helpful for kids who have more severe symptoms of ADHD. The American Academy of Pediatrics states that the primary treatment for ADHD in young children should be behavioural therapy.

This method, also known as behavioural modification, focuses on addressing certain harmful behaviours and provides solutions to their prevention. It may also include establishing expectations and guidelines for the youngster. It may be a potent tool in assisting your kid since behavioural therapy and medicine work best together.

Parenting counseling may help parents get the necessary resources to support their ADHD child's success. Long-term benefits may be achieved for both the kid and the parent by arming parents with the methods and approaches necessary to deal with behavioural issues.

4. Avoid using food dyes and preservatives

Certain symptoms of ADHD may be managed with the use of alternative therapies, such as:

• Regularly being interrupted by forgetting
• Organizational issues
• Inability to pay attention,

Certain preservatives and food colourings may make some kids more hyperactive. Preservatives and colourings in these foods should be avoided:

• Sundown yellow, or FD&C Yellow No. 6, may be found in soft drinks, confectionery, frosting, and cereal.

• Pickles, granola bars, cereal, and yoghurt all contain FD&C Yellow No. 5 (tartrazine).

• Salad dressings, fruit juice products, and carbonated drinks all include the chemical sodium benzoate.

• Quinoline yellow, or D&C Yellow No. 10, may be found in sorbets, juices, and

smoked haddock.
• FD&C Red No. 40 (Allura red), which is present in ice cream, children's pharmaceuticals, sweets made with gelatin, and soft beverages.

5. Examine EEG biofeedback

Brain wave measurements are used in electroencephalographic (EEG) biofeedback, a Neurotherapy. According to 2011 research, EEG training has promise as a therapy for ADHD.

A youngster could engage in a unique video game during a normal session. They'll be assigned a job to focus on, like maintaining the plane's flight. If they get disoriented, the aircraft will begin to descend, or the display will go black. Throughout time, the game gradually teaches the kid new concentrating skills. The youngster will eventually learn to recognise and treat their symptoms.

6. Being in the fresh air

Children with ADHD may benefit from spending time outdoors. There is compelling evidence that even 20 minutes spent outdoors may help children by enhancing their focus. The best environments are those surrounded by greenery and wildlife.

The notion that frequent exposure to the outdoors with green space can be a natural and secure therapy that may be utilised to aid persons with ADHD is supported by 2011 research and other studies that came before it.

9.2 Pet Therapy

Those battling various mental health conditions, such as anxiety and depression, or individuals who feel lonely might benefit from emotional support animals. Whereas it remains a novel concept, owning a pet may make individuals with ADHD happier and better for their mental health.

With all the illogical and bizarre treatments mentioned, acquiring a cute dog does not seem too horrible. Adopting a dog is a decision that should be carefully considered, but dogs may be a good addition to the lives of individuals with ADHD.

9.3 The Best Dog Breed

When buying a new dog, many individuals frequently pick a breed in mind, which makes them assume that the only place to purchase their dog will be a breeder. But did you realize many purebred and mixed-breed dogs are also at shelters? Various shelters are available, providing many options when choosing a breed. The gratitude a rescue dog will feel for being given a second opportunity at life can offer an ADHD sufferer quite a great feeling of fulfilment, regardless of whether you choose a mongrel or a designer breed. Because of their deep, unconditional affection and whatever past experiences they may have, rescue dogs can provide a surprising amount of assistance. The types you like the most are the finest dog breeds for ADHD!

9.4 Cognitive behavioural therapy in children with ADHD (CBT)

Cognitive behavioural therapy (CBT) helps you recognise negative beliefs and replace them with positive ones. The foundation of CBT is that your thoughts influence your emotions, which in turn influence your actions. It's simple to get into a negative thinking and action habit. With CBT, you may recognise these tendencies and alter them. For instance, you can be worried that you won't be able to accomplish a significant project for work or school on time since it has a deadline.

For many persons with ADHD, cognitive behavioural therapy is a successful treatment. You may explore your mental patterns in this treatment and reorganise them to be more beneficial. You may treat many ADHD symptoms using this method. It has been shown that CBT and medicine work better together than medication alone. Even after therapy sessions are over, CBT may still have positive benefits.

9.5 Counseling and Education Services

Parents must be conscious of the many supports, adjustments, and special services available to assist their ADHD kid in achieving academic success.
The educational system must identify and evaluate children who may have difficulties. You may seek an assessment for your kid at any time as a parent.
In addition to speaking with your child's teacher and the school administrator, it is often beneficial to place the request in writing.
A mental or physical impairment that significantly restricts one or more key living activities qualifies as a disability for students. As studying is seen as a significant living activity, many ADHD kids have been deemed "persons with disabilities" under Section 504.

To offer special education support and services in the least restrictive setting, ADHD students often stay in their normal classrooms while receiving the necessary adjustments and accommodations instead of being put in a different special needs classroom. Only if the kid continues to struggle sufficiently in the normal classroom after modifications and interventions will removal from the regular mainstream classroom occur.

Innovative therapies for ADHD

9.6 Music Therapy

ADHD sufferers often have a lot of mental and physical energy. Their minds race at breakneck speed, making it challenging to calm down, focus on one item at a time, or maintain long-term attention on a single job. According to 2020 research, youngsters with ADHD seemed to concentrate and pay more attention while listening to music.

People with ADHD benefit from music therapy because they seek the kind of structure music offers. Music therapy songs have definite beginnings, middles, and finishes and are predictable. Also, the beats and rhythms have defined structures that might aid in better mental organisation and increase concentration.

9.7 Equine Therapy

It may be challenging for parents and teachers of children with ADHD to handle normal circumstances. Every day is challenging when dealing with a disgruntled youngster, but there is no hope. Equine therapy, particularly simulators, allows you to enjoy the therapeutic advantages of horseback riding without caring for or maintaining a real animal. It enables your kid to unwind and maintain their composure, which is advantageous for them in every sphere of life.

The horse moves in a rhythmic manner (or simulator). Children have better posture, mobility, balance, and coordination. Finally, balance and coordination issues might affect kids with ADHD. It could make them anxious or furious, causing them to slump out and not straighten up. They settle down as a result of those repetitive motions and must sit up taller to prevent falling. Youngsters must train themselves to move with confidence and attention to this.

9.8 Art Therapy

A tool that offers a non-verbal method of communication and emotional expression is art therapy. The act of making art stimulates the brain, increasing dopamine levels. Elevated dopamine levels enhance attention, which is crucial for those with ADHD (Attention Deficit Hyperactivity Disorder). Besides increasing serotonin and lowering stress levels, creative expression via the arts. When used therapeutically, producing art may also help adults and kids with ADHD, tips and particularly children with learning difficulties and dyslexic children's motor skills.

9.9 Guided Meditation

Treatment and medication are effective strategies to control your ADHD symptoms. Nevertheless, these are not your only choices. According to recent research, mindfulness meditation, which involves paying attention to your thoughts and emotions as they arise, may also help you concentrate better and relax your mind. Your capacity to direct your attention is strengthened through mindfulness meditation.

It trains you to be aware of your thoughts and concentrate. Also, it teaches you how to focus on the present moment again after being distracted. Also, it might help you become more conscious of your feelings, so you're less prone to react rashly. Do you think about too many things? Imagine a sky that is blue featuring fluffy white clouds. The clouds stand in for your ideas, while the sky symbolises your consciousness. To refocus, pay attention to the brief gaps in the clouds. A walking meditation might be equally as effective as a seated meditation if you have problems sitting still.

Gently return your focus to the feelings on the bottoms of your feet whenever your thoughts stray. Create some signals that encourage habit formation. Put a reminder on your phone or note it in your calendar to remember you at a specified time. Similar to how having a workout partner may simplify exercising, finding a yoga or meditation partner can help you persist.

CHAPTER 10

ADHD Medications for Children

10.1 The Most Popular Medications for Children

You should understand how stimulants, such as amphetamine or methylphenidate, plus non-stimulants function, as well as any potential hazards, as well as recommended doses and frequency if you're thinking about giving your kid ADHD medication.

i. Concerta (methylphenidate)
ii. Focalin XR (methylphenidate)
iii. Ritalin (methylphenidate)
iv. Vyvanse (lisdexamfetamine dimesylate)
v. Adderall XR (amphetamine)
vi. Evekeo (amphetamine)
vii. Quillivant XR (methylphenidate)
viii. Strattera (atomoxetine hydrochloride)

While using a stimulant drug like methylphenidate (Ritalin, Concerta, Metadate, Quillivant XR, Adhansia XR, Jornay P.M, etc.) or amphetamine, the majority of children with ADHD see an improvement in their symptoms (Adderall, Dynavel XR, Dexedrine, Adzenys XR, etc.). The doctor may recommend a different prescription if an ADHD medication doesn't appear to function or only works when taken in excessively high dosages.

10.2 How does It Work?

ADHD medications increase attention by enhancing the function of normal brain chemicals. Dopamine and norepinephrine, two brain neurotransmitters, are the focus of the medications. These substances have an impact on concentration and focus.

Depending on the type, different ways of working with ADHD medications. Yet, the way that all ADHD drugs operate is by raising the number of vital neurotransmitters in the brain. These neurotransmitters consist of norepinephrine and dopamine. Enhancing attention span is one of the symptoms of ADHD that is improved by increasing these neurotransmitters.

- Managing impulsive actions
- Lowering excessive activities
- The control of executive dysfunction

Each individual is affected by ADHD meds differently. What is beneficial for one individual may not be for the kid or you. It's also possible that the initial ADHD medication kids or you take aren't the best. It may not work, or it could have unfavourable side effects. Alternatively, you could be on the right drug but require a bigger dosage.

Tell your doctor about all the drugs you or your kid are taking, whether prescription or over-the-counter. Moreover, tell your doctor whether you drink coffee or take any supplements and how much you take daily. Mixing certain drugs might be detrimental to health.

To discover the right prescription and dosage for you or your kid, your healthcare provider could have to experiment with several drugs and dosages. Your healthcare practitioner will monitor you or your kid and change the medication's dosage to strike the ideal balance between its advantages and disadvantages.

Most patients find that ADHD medication reduces symptoms after discovering the proper dosage and medicine. Attention span, hyperactivity, and impulsive behaviour problems go better.

10.3 Are They Necessary?

Not all children with ADHD need medication. But, medication may often improve a child's ability to concentrate, listen, and fidget for longer periods. Children may learn and practise skills like keeping organised or waiting their time without interrupting via behavioural therapy.

10.4 What Are the Benefits?

The primary line of therapy for ADHD is medication. According to studies, they successfully treat 80% of affected youngsters. But, you could be concerned about the medication's adverse effects or wish to avoid taking it for another reason.

One of the numerous advantages of treating ADHD is that it may prolong life. A person can better manage their chronic health conditions and prevent the onset of co-occurring disorders by getting treatment for ADHD. Improved health management may extend life by nine to thirteen years.

We discovered that ADHD negatively impacts every facet of life satisfaction and longevity after evaluating the long-term health effects of the disorder. It is because ADHD sufferers naturally struggle with self-regulation, which results in poor self-care & impulsive, dangerous behaviour. The results are alarming but also reassuring because ADHD represents the most easily managed mental health condition in psychiatry.

Properly managing ADHD symptoms could aid a child's academic success, friendship and social development, and family life.

The protective advantages include preventing substance use, disruptive behaviours, and early sexual activity, as well as safeguarding and fostering a positive sense of oneself and confidence. Teenagers taking medication as part of their therapy have adequate driving records and experience fewer vehicular mishaps.

10.5 Are There Any Side Effects?

Appetite loss and sleep issues are the most frequent adverse effects. Furthermore, jitteriness, moodiness, irritability, headaches, rapid heartbeat, stomachaches, and elevated blood pressure are adverse effects of ADHD medications. Side effects often manifest in the initial few days after beginning a new medication or using a higher dosage.

10.6 Learn about Stimulants for children

Dopamine and norepinephrine are two important neurochemicals to remember while discussing stimulant drugs for ADHD therapy. Both are crucial for the pre-frontal cortex area of the brain to operate properly in terms of attention and concentration. Consider it the brain's secretary: It's where executive functioning, or how you organise, plan, and carry out your tasks, occurs.

Dopamine is important for reducing signals from external stimuli, which could be distracting, while norepinephrine is important for enhancing the signal you're attempting to concentrate on or pay attention to. Adderall, Ritalin, or any other type of stimulant medicine helps raise the levels of norepinephrine and dopamine in the body.
You are fairly concentrated if your dopamine and norepinephrine levels are appropriate. Nevertheless, you risk stressing out your brain if you have too much. Then, you nearly seem as if your ADHD is worse. Teenagers, in particular, think that if something is nice at this dosage, it will only improve with more. Not at all. You can get worse symptoms and a lot of negative side effects. The goal is to strive to strike the proper balance.

Several stimulant prescription choices are available for ADHD, but they are not all equal. Different formulations may elicit quite varied reactions in children.

10.7 Short-Acting or Long-Acting Stimulants?

Short-Acting Stimulants
The oldest of them all, **Ritalin**, is a methylphenidate formulation with a short half-life of 3–4 hours. Another methylphenidate variant that lasts for roughly 4 hours is **Focalin**. Around 30 to 45 minutes after administering any of these drugs, they start to function.
 This drug may be crumbled and blended with food for kids with difficulty swallowing tablets. The chewable tablet and liquid forms of the brief methylphenidate are also available.
Regarding amphetamines, **Adderall, Zenzedi, Evekeo, and Dexedrine** are short-acting varieties that work approximately 30 to 45 minutes after use and last 3 to 4 hours. The effects of amphetamines are generally comparable to those of methylphenidate; however, they tend to be a bit stronger and stay a little longer.

Long-Acting Stimulants

Similar to methylphenidate, various formulations of amphetamines were deve-loped to release the drug more slowly, lengthening the time it takes for the tre-atment to take action. It is quite helpful when attempting to provide an answer that lasts the whole school day, usually 6 to 8 hours. Some of these substances start working as rapidly as the short-acting versions of these drugs.

The primary element in Adderall, amphetamine, is attached to an additional sub-stance called lysine in Vyvanse, adding a second step for the body to take to bre-ak it off and make it active. Hence, **Vyvanse** has an extremely long half-life of up to 14 hours. It could be too long for a seven-year-old, but it might be fantastic if you're in high school, college, or as an adult. It's merely a powdered medication; there are no beads. Yet the discharge will be steady, with no peaks or valleys.

The longer-acting variety, **Adderall XR**, is intended to work for 10–12 hours. It is a capsule containing beads split 50/50, meaning that 50% is released imme-diately, and another 50% is released later. The beads may be removed from the capsule and combined with food.

The stable version of **Dexedrine** is available as a capsule and normally lasts 6 to 8 hours.
Adzenys XR-ODT is an orally disintegrating tablet that doesn't need swallowing. Its reaction time is between 10 and 12 hours.
Amphetamine comes in a stable liquid version called **Dynavel XR**. Its effects may last for up to 10 to 12 hours.

10.8 What are the common side effects associated with ADHD medication?

Early on in the course of drug therapy for ADHD, side effects are possible. Most of the time, these negative consequences are minor and transient. During the initial weeks of therapy, they can go away as your body becomes used to the drug. They may sometimes be extremely severe or persist longer. The following are some of the adverse effects of ADHD medications:

Reduced Appetite: Around 80% of stimulant drug patients have decreased ap-petite.

Inability to sleep: You could have a harder time getting to sleep and staying asleep. Overall, you could have a less restful sleep. Taking your medicines throughout the day, particularly those with prolonged release might assist in lessening this adverse effect.

Loss of weight: If you take your medicine after meals and include protein drinks or snacks in your diet, you could be able to control any unexpected weight loss. Additional adverse effects of ADHD medication include the following.

Rebounding impact: a brief period of increased activity, weariness, or depression when the medicine wears off.

Tics. Sudden, repeated motions or noises, such as throat clearing or eye blinking: Tics are not caused by ADHD medication, although they may render them more obvious than they would be otherwise.

Anxiety: Anxiety and despair, either new or worsening.

A little delay in development: Some youngsters who use stimulants suffer a growth slowdown, although it does not impact their eventual height.

Heart rate and blood pressure variations: Blood pressure may increase or decrease depending on the drug. Your heart rate may also slightly rise if you use stimulant drugs. The rise is often slight and not harmful, but if you or your kid have a history of cardiac issues, you should let your healthcare professional know.

Uneasy stomach: Throwing up and nausea may be part of this.

Changes in drug dose or schedule may be used to manage side effects that persist after several weeks of therapy.

• Use a different stimulant drug
• Switching to an extended-release dosage type
• Attempting a non-stimulant drug

CHAPTER 11

Positive Parenting Strategies

11.1 Strategies for Managing Emotions

Emotion regulation is our capacity to exert sufficient control over emotional reactions. While an inability to control one's emotions is not a sign of ADHD, people with the disorder often feel overwhelmed or swamped with emotions. Intense and powerful emotions may sometimes have advantageous effects, such as being enthusiastic about a family vacation, but they can also make it difficult to get through the day.

Learning how to control your emotions is possible, often with the assistance of adults such as parents.

These are some methods that might be useful at work or school:

• Discuss your emotions when it is acceptable.
• Exemplify emotional control. What techniques do you employ when you're anxious or frustrated?
• Nearly the same amount of consistency as you can muster Children's physical and emotional development depends on regular mealtimes and bedtimes.
• Encourage your kids to express their emotions through conversation. When emotions are mentioned in literature or television, label your child's sentiments and discuss them.
• Breathe deeply by practising. The entire family can use this tool, which may be

utilised anywhere!

11.2 Tips to Improve the Parent-Child Relationship: The Stick and the Carrot?

Several parenting techniques are beneficial for kids with ADHD. As their brains function differently, other family members often need to make some modifications. Take better care of your kid by using these tried-and-true methods. Utilize these methods to assist your youngster every day.

Family support for children with ADHD

Structure

Structure enables children with ADHD to comprehend expectations and appropriate behaviour. For their everyday life, they need precisely defined routines. Keep your child's life structured using timetables and calendars; older children may also utilise clocks and timers. Structure helps your youngster concentrate on tasks by reducing disarray and distractions. Establish times for routines. Add time slots for preparing for class, schoolwork, having fun, and retiring to bed. Invite your kid to help build the construction. Please make a list of chores, for instance, that they may cross off when they are completed. Make it enjoyable and provide rewards that must be earned. Give them some leeway to express their ideas and, when necessary, push the limits.

Encourage Speaking aloud

ADHD symptoms often include poor impulse control. Your youngster could act or say something out of the blue. Urge them to speak more slowly and honestly. It may teach kids to think about the effects of their words and deeds. They may then choose whether or not to follow through. Also, this may assist you, and other adults in comprehending your child's mental processes. While you listen, get a deeper understanding of how their mind functions.

Establish a calming environment

Even more so for a youngster with an attention deficit, a child's bedroom ought to provide a place for them to unwind and rest. Provide their room with a tranquil space. Use technology sparingly in the bedroom. These gadgets may prevent your kid from getting the rest they need to control their energy levels. Refrain from being distracted by excess toys or posters. Think about using soothing colours to paint your walls. Until the youngster is older, avoid adding a desk. Desks may become disorganised, which can be stressful.

Exercise is encouraged

Energy levels in ADHD children are often high. Please give them a lot of things to do and exercise. Exercise may give your kid a constructive outlet for their energy and interests and help them focus and concentrate better.
Pick a hobby your children like, and encourage as much outside time as possible. Participate actively and whenever you can. Hiking together as a family may strengthen your bonds.

Remain calm

Always try to maintain your composure. Even though you may sometimes get upset, fighting serves no one. Your youngster could follow your lead if you lose your composure. Have a positive dialogue, build a relationship with your kid, and work together to find a solution. Say something like, "I realise you don't find this entertaining," rather than becoming aggressive, and then follow up with "positive expectations" and a kind pat on the shoulder. Recognize that problems are challenging for your kid as well. Do these calming hobbies in your free time to keep yourself calm. Take a minute to pause, inhale deeply, and count to 10 before reacting to agitated or assertive behaviour.

Maintain expectations

The greatest results for ADHD children occur when expectations are made explicit. Create a list of expectations for behaviour and objectives to assist your youngster in understanding what is expected. Be consistent; uncertainty in how rules are applied leads to misunderstanding. Always follow through if a reward is offered or when punishment is called for.

Employ Reward-Based Training

"The carrot" is usually more effective than "the stick." Punishment seldom produces the same effects as positive reinforcement, such as hugs or valuable time with you. Stay away from offensive words and actions. Raising your voice is one strategy that often fails. Children with ADHD may have trouble controlling their emotions. Your advice is what kids depend on to understand what to do. They could try to match your level of emotion if you are upset. Acknowledge your child's accomplishments.
As a reward for excellent behaviour, provide special rights like a special excursion

with you. If you must institute penalties for bad behaviour, ensure the reaction is prompt, predictable, and constant. Any punishment should be proportionate to the child's age and the seriousness of the behaviour.

Do not be distracted

Provide children with ADHD with a setting that can keep them engaged since they like diversions that are simple to reach. Establish a distraction-free workspace for your homework. Organise their schoolwork and responsibilities to prevent youngsters from being overburdened with labour. To help them, provide a specific time limit for each assignment. While working on lengthier jobs, plan frequent breaks. Create a plan of action and divide the job into smaller tasks for bigger projects.

Build a Team

Consider your family to be a team. Spend quality time with your kid and work on improving your relationship. You'll be able to communicate more effectively as a result of this. Ensure you and the other adults that engage with your kid work together in a coordinated manner.

Everyone involved in a child's care and education must agree on the child's treatment and objectives. Sharing critical information via coordination enables everyone to assist one another and contribute to a unified strategy in the event of any behavioural challenges.

Since every kid is unique, try various approaches to see what works best for you and the child. For aid with parenting techniques and to ensure your child's success, speak with qualified therapists.

11.3 Help Him Build Proper Trust

Have faith in your kid. Make a mental or written list of your kid's wonderful, priceless, and distinctive qualities. Have faith in your child's capacity to grow, adapt, and achieve. Every day while you prepare your coffee or wash your teeth, remind yourself of this trust.

11.4 Help Him Build a Proper Self-Esteem

Regularly giving your kid unfavourable criticism might damage their self-esteem. Praise your kid for their accomplishments in two steps while acknowledging and emphasising their difficulties. Acknowledge wins, no matter how little, and explain to your youngster why it was successful.

Describe any mental or emotional obstacles he may have faced and how he overcame them to thrive in this situation. Determine your child's abilities, note any lingering worries
they may have after school, and ensure they can succeed when engaging in these activities. Don't ruin the enjoyment by denying him his favourite pastimes as "compensation" for doing something he dislikes.

Personal growth for children with ADHD

By dividing tasks into manageable, incremental components or stages, you may assist your kid in completing challenging activities. Establish a regular special time with your kid to strengthen healthy bonding and protect them from attacks on their self-worth. Invite a classmate over for a monitored play date and engage in social skills role-playing with your youngster. Remind your youngster that they have your unwavering affection and backing. Acknowledge the challenges they confront and let them know you adore them.

11.5 How To Motivate ADHD brains

The motivation of the ADHD brain differs from that of neurotypical brains. The words "should" and "ought to" not affect it. Instead of hearing "It would be better if," it reacts to the current situation. How about at this very moment? Staying stationary always feels better than moving.

Interest/Passion

How ADHDer hasn't heard the phrase "Why can you yet you can't do" from themselves or a loved one? That could be perplexing. If you start doing something that interests you and replaces it with something else that doesn't give you the same sense of intrinsic joy or motivation, the train will come to a grinding stop. The ADHD brain is activated by interest and enthusiasm. It stimulates the mind and draws it in the direction of that interest. It implies that when you are engaged in a task, the initiation barrier that prevents you from beginning acts like a very soft speed bump—you may not even be aware of its presence. Yet, a work with little interest? The first obstacle may equally well be a two-story wall. It seems almost impossible to scale, given the power needed.

Novelty

There aren't many things more alluring than something brand-new and gleaming. Our brains are wired to seek novelty; this is part of what aids in learning and keeps us secure.

The same attraction to the book exists in the ADHD brain but is shown with much more intensity and fervour. Therefore, what are the new duties, connections, and projects? They all energise and ignite the ADHD brain. Novelty ignites the curious, youthful learner who yearns to explore, acquire knowledge, and develop. It stimulates the mind and gets your creative juices flowing. The dopamine that the brain receives from this stimulation keeps it active.

Pressure

We all carry a motivator in our back pockets that we may use as required: pressure. It is the most straightforward to produce and one item you can often depend on.

The paper due tomorrow, your boss demanding the report it was due three weeks ago, and your wife sobbing over a missed anniversary are all examples of pressure.

Since it's the simplest to produce, it's the incentive employed most often. Not in the mood to begin that program right now? Waiting a few weeks or hours until the deadline will seem more appealing.

Competition

Competitiveness activates the ADHD brain. As a result, the initiation barrier is essentially destroyed. It gets it fired up and active, and then all of a quick, the battle is about succeeding rather than beginning.

Some psychological elements may make competition grind, perhaps an ADHD brain to a standstill. But not everyone reacts well to competition. Hence, you are not isolated if this doesn't work for you. Yet it may be a powerful motivation for such brains that do react.

11.6 How Do You Get Your Kid to Do Chores without Arguing

Focusing on one task at a time, making alternative plans for intervention, and seeming certain and serious are all ways to persuade our kids to accomplish tasks without nagging and fighting with them. Being excellent actors and refraining from nagging, demanding, or shouting is crucial since doing so will surprise our children. Instead, try explaining, "Your obligation this week is simply to clean the dishes before you enjoy any TV tonight," gently and firmly. By doing this, you and your kid can establish reasonable goals, stick to them, and finally achieve them.

Potential growth in children with ADHD

For instance, we may state, "Instead of bugging and fighting, "We're going right now, and we have to leave so that I can finish the tasks for today. I'll have to devote the time away from your computer time if you cause us to be late.

"Please don't eat that food again, or we'll be forced to leave the shop and go home. Now, we can be open with our kids about why they won't receive the Christmas present we planned for them
 They will learn from this that we're serious and that boundaries and structure make people feel safer. Once we succeed and learn that we can influence our children's conduct without resorting to nagging, we may also become more at ease.

Decide in advance what you will say and when and where you will say it. Say, "We're now to tell you everything we expect of you," during a family gathering. Make sure your kids understand that they are all responsible family members. If you have problems establishing your power as a parent, arrange where you sit to indicate that you're in command. A single mother intended to give her kids clear, realistic expectations at dinner after dessert, establishing a foundation for future pleasant interactions and a healthier connection with her kids. Be explicit about penalties for not performing tasks and create age-appropriate punishments if the kids don't carry through.

You might want to assist young kids or youngsters who are unorganised in tackling a task. A chore schedule or a list of items they need to accomplish to complete the assignment might also be useful. It is essential to remember that establishing expectations for the kids and keeping them responsible is to develop them into accountable and productive members of society. Nagging and fighting didn't improve your getting to your objective, but having realistic expectations and keeping through the will.

11.7 The Chore Chart That Motivates Your Child

Make chore charts for youngsters basic. Try to visualise the chore chart from your child's viewpoint. If it's difficult to stare at, consider what your youngster sees! Thus they should be simple to look at and comprehend. Less is more once it involves making things attractive for youngsters with ADHD. Too much glitter, bright colours, or stickers may quickly overwhelm or distract toddlers with visual processing trouble. Keep colours plain and lettering bold and readable.

One highly effective chore chart concept is constructing a chart with huge, unmissable language.

Here's an instance of how to construct a clear, usable, Homemade chart:

Step 1: Put duties into a Word document
Step 2: Change the font and font size for maximum readability, i.e. Arial Black
Step 3: Printing it out
Step 4: Laminate your paper
Step 5: Split each job into horizontal strips
Step 6: Attach Velcro command strips towards the back of chores and your chore chart

Not only may your duties be changed on the go, but they should also be friendlier in the eyes.

Ideas for chore charts for children ages 4 to 6
1. Clean up the kitchen table.
2. Feed domestic animals
3. Gather any stray toys and reposition them in the toy box or shelf.
4. hydrate indoor plants
5. Place your shoes on the rack or in the shoe bin

Ideas for chore charts for children aged 5 to 8
1. Delete the dishwasher
2. Dishwasher load
3. Organize the groceries
4. Unload the dryer
5. Window and doorknob cleaning

Ideas for chore charts for children aged 9 to 11
1. Clean flooring
2. Remove garbage
3. Start and load the washer
4. towel folds
5. Vacuum floors

Ideas for chore charts for kids 12 and up
1. Clean flooring
2. Make straightforward meals or sides.
3. monitoring younger siblings
4. pet walk
5. wash the vehicle

CHAPTER 12

ADHD and Sport

12.1 The Best Sport for ADHD?

For your kid with ADHD, choosing the correct sport or activity may significantly improve attention, mood, and self-esteem. While it has been shown that exercise may help manage ADHD symptoms, neither all sports are made equal. Some sports could be better for your kid than others, depending on their particular combination of symptoms.

These are 10 sports that parents, coaches, and specialists suggest for kids with ADHD.

Martial arts: Teaches discipline and respect.
Gymnastics: Improves awareness and attention.
Soccer: Fosters a feeling of community among children with ADHD.
Cross-country and track: Teach discipline and pace.
Baseball: Teaches sportsmanship and patience.
Swimming: Gives ADHD kids structure and direction.
Tennis: Offers individualised competition.
Wrestling: A constructive outlet for emotions.
Riding a horse: Teaches children to mimic their horse's behavioural changes.
Archery: Teaches discipline and laser-like concentration.

Consider the importance of the coaches before choosing a sport. Most coaches are well-intentioned parents who have little knowledge of ADHD, but a compassionate coach may make a big difference.

12.2 How motor activity develops social-cognitive and learning skills

Many kids with ADHD exhibit motor impairments during everyday activities, which may affect their growth. Children having ADHD who have motor difficulties may exhibit impairments while doing movements-intensive activities like handwriting.

Many youngsters with ADHD are found to have motor deficits. Children with certain fine motor deficits may struggle in school, have poor self-esteem, and feel frustrated. Despite these extensive effects, the population with ADHD has remained severely undertreated for fine motor deficits.

The use of particular fine motor & cognitive training components, a combination of feedback mechanisms, physical exercise, or multimodal therapies is all effective ways to improve fine motor skills in children with ADHD. Instruction programs must be adapted to the unique characteristics of the population with ADHD.

Even though they are often present in children having ADHD, fine motor deficits have largely gone untreated up to this point. There is a critical need for non-pharmacological therapies designed specifically for people with ADHD and adapted to their unique requirements. The examination of successful therapies for children with ADHD who have fine-motor challenges has made hopeful progress by the current scoping review. In the long and short term, a range of training regimens and intensity seems useful. The most successful approaches for treating the disease seem to include a variety of modalities, verbal or automated feedback, and compelling serious games.

Contrary to the opinions of some, writing by hand and having fine motor control will still be valuable life skills in the digital age, and the latter offers a wide range of possibilities for the therapies of motor comorbidities as well as for future studies in an interdisciplinary area involving occupational therapy, psychology, hand gaming. Outside their laboratory, a fascinating new world awaits psychologists, asking them to delve into the world of serious playing to create efficient training interventions.

12.3 The Coach and the Team

According to research, clients of ADHD coaching have improvements in their executive function abilities, self-esteem, and self-efficacy.

Most ADHD sufferers gain by having the chance to vocally process during coaching sessions.

ADHD coaching aids in overcoming overload and immobility.

Using chances for verbal processing, reducing overload, accountability, and body doubling, ADHD coaching produces positive client results. The importance of coaching as a crucial component of therapy is getting more widely acknowledged as we move to multimodal treatment methods for ADHD.

A skilled coach may help you achieve your objectives by assisting you to grow.

• Improved connections and self-esteem
• A higher feeling of self-efficacy
• Time management abilities
• Talents in organization and management
• Improved judgment
• Self-motivation

12.4 Individual or Team Sports?

Some hyperactive children having ADHD do well in sports that demand individual concentration, like solo sports in which the coach may provide them with more individualised focus to assist them in concentrating on one activity. Examples include wrestling, tennis, field and track, martial arts, and swimming.

Although more each time must be beneficial, your kid could lose out on a few sports' team socialising, collaboration, and friendship-building advantages. But, if your youngster is easily swayed within a group setting, solitary sports can be the best option.

Yet if your kid is keen on participating in the team sport, parents should support them in doing that. Team sports provide opportunities to practise some social skills, which some ADHD children find difficult. Team sports have been reported to help certain ADHD sufferers with social skill deficiencies.

12.5 Outdoor or Indoor Sports?

Both outdoor and indoor sports have advantages, but some evidence indicates that people with ADHD may benefit much of exercising in all-natural settings.

For instance, team sports like basketball and soccer need continual movement and competition. In contrast, there may be higher waiting around inside plays in baseball, which raises the likelihood of a distraction.

All sports with many rules, plays, and strategy requirements may be too much for your youngster to handle. Children with ADHD often do better once there is a clear objective, such as swimming to the pool end, despite condition-based sports, such as changing plays in football.

Teamwork and good peer connections are two key advantages of sports teams. A win-win situation is when your youngster engages in physical activity while having fun along their buddies. A sports team also lessens the burden on your kid personally since you lose and win together.

The sport your kid ultimately chooses to participate in will depend on their particular personality, tastes, and medical diagnoses.

CHAPTER 13

ADHD, What kinds Of Games

13.1 Serious Games for ADHD child

Patients with ADHD may benefit greatly from using serious games, a new technology. In contrast to conventional approaches, gamifying the diagnostic and treatment procedure with serious games might not only make ADHD in youngsters more enjoyable but also lessen symptoms. The conduct of the players is tracked, and certain data gathered may be used to diagnose ADHD properly. Machine learning technology can also categorise game data to identify ADHD patients. Children with ADHD may benefit from various training effects from various game mechanics and operating techniques. These games have contributed to developing executive functions, social communication abilities, and attention in children with ADHD.

Electronic games substantially pique the attention of kids with ADHD since they may provide players with vivid game sceneries and immediate rewards.
The ability of video games to imitate actual events is crucial, and as augmented virtual reality and reality advance, kids with ADHD may be put in more realistic gaming environments. Based on their actions and responses in the game makes it easier to diagnose and treat them. The training effects obtained in the game are also simpler to apply to real life.

13.2 Toys

A lack of concentration, impulsivity and hyperactivity in adults and children cha-
racterises an attention-deficit/hyperactivity disorder (ADHD) diagnosis. A good
method to redirect some of those behaviours is using sensory toys, which are
becoming more popular within and outside the mental health community. These
toys may have soothing or grounding effects by giving
individuals something to do and directing wandering attention as fidgeting with
a tactile, simple activity. These may lessen feelings of boredom emotions as well.

13.3 Video Games

Although there is unquestionably a link between ADHD plus video games, it is
not a cause-and-effect relationship. Those with ADHD could be more likely to engage in problematic gaming activities. The chance increases as a person's symptoms become more severe.
Video game playing has a wide range of advantages, according to studies.
Video game play may increase:

• Another use for video games is as a tool for measuring and studying.
• Children are taught social skills and problem-solving

Despite being a fairly recent trend, mounting evidence suggests video games
may be effective aids for controlling ADHD.
Just 1 game, EndeavorRX, has been given FDA approval as a prescription video
game.
Like other types of entertainment, video games are a component of popular culture. Although children experiencing ADHD are more likely to engage in dangerous gaming habits, most kids limit their video game time to reasonable amoun-
ts.

13.4 Teach the Rules as You Play

Set time constraints. Schedule one 10-minute play session each day; longer sessions increase the chance of the youngster losing interest and the adult losing
patience. Use toys as props, and recommend developing a narrative centred
around the figurine or toy.

Encourage your youngster. Once upon a time, let your youngster make up and
perform the rest of the narrative. You may engage with your child's character by

taking on one of the parts in the scenario.

Promote social interaction. Engage in interactions with your kid that help him practise social skills, understand logical implications, and ultimately predict outcomes. Say something like, "What will the girl must play with if she smashes all her toys?" Children having ADHD are so accustomed to receiving discipline that they may respond to a warning more readily if it is not personal to them.

Whenever required, reroute. When your kid strays from the game, gently nudge her in the right direction by saying, "I was very fascinated in that horsey tale. Please explain what occurs next.

Finish the process. After ten minutes, if the youngster hasn't concluded their imagination, urge them by saying things like, "Well, it's becoming dark. "The boy's mother is summoning him to return home for supper right now," or "Time for horsey to be ready for bed." Give the narrative one more minute, then put the toys away.

You'll probably see an improvement in your child's capacity to persevere with the work after a few months. At a certain point, you may progressively increase the difficulty by creating more complex themes and even changing the game's location from the playroom floor across your home.

13.5 How to Help Him Grow With Fun

You may engage in activities to help your kid concentrate on something enjoyable and strengthen your relationship with them. Finding entertainment for your youngster isn't required to be difficult. Instead, even if you're merely cooking or doing tasks around the home, try to find ways to infuse excitement and adventure into your day! These enjoyable activities for
children with ADHD may help them find a necessary outlet for their energy and provide you and your child valuable family time.

Build something
ADHD is only one of the numerous mental health issues that may benefit from creative expression. For instance, expressive art therapy may benefit adults and children with ADHD. C Focus, communication, focus, and problem-solving abilities are just a few talents that could help youngsters develop and practise. Also, it may help with stress management, self-awareness development, and emotional expression.

Engage in adventure
Considering children with ADHD often experience boredom, providing new activities may be a fantastic approach to keep them engaged.

Work together on a project
Together, working on the project may be a pleasant way to strengthen your relationship with your kid and support their ability to concentrate.

Cook collectively
For children with ADHD, cooking is a fantastic hobby since it engages various senses. Also, it's a pleasant method to strengthen your relationship with your kid and impart useful life lessons. Before moving on to more complicated recipes, start with simple ones that are excellent for beginners.

Go to it!
Take a stroll, ride bikes, or play tag with your companions. Moving their bodies can help your youngster concentrate their energy on an enjoyable and fulfilling activity.

Set up a system
Many children with ADHD have trouble staying organised, but it may be enjoyable if you turn to organise and clean up into a game.

Perform Games
Word games, memory games, or even interactive games involving musical chairs are excellent for some children.

Leave the house now
Sometimes leaving home is the greatest option for keeping an ADHD youngster entertained. Make arrangements for a day excursion to a location where your youngster will be interested. It may be a new playground, a zoo, an amusement park, or perhaps a museum.

Observe the stars
Children of all ages may enjoy the peaceful hobby of stargazing. It's a wonderful opportunity to spend time with your kid and educate them about science and their surroundings.

13.6 ADHD Gadgets

Puzzler's Cube
The traditional Rubik's Cube is a great toy for ADHD because of its vivid colours and properly hand-sized shape. This 3D toy combines physical feeling with aesthetic appeal and problem-solving abilities, which may aid focus and attention span development.

Changing-Shape Boxes
The relaxing, therapeutic benefits of shape-shifting puzzle boxes may make individuals feel more at ease, rooted, and focused. They are magnetic puzzle boxes that you can modify and reconfigure into different geometric forms.
Some provide extra stimulation by incorporating sensory elements and aesthetically arresting designs.

Magnesium balls
Magnet balls aren't exactly like stress balls; they're more like shape-shifting box puzzles in that you can change their form and appearance. A collection of tiny, magnetic balls known as "magnet balls" are magnetically drawn to one another. Just rotating and pulling the balls allows users to construct their unique design, which may help them concentrate and calm down.

Motion Sandscape with Liquid
Liquid motion sandscapes are interactive works of art that resemble dunes visually and aurally. These are intended to be turned and flipped, which causes the sand within to move mesmerizingly and produce a new pattern. You may choose from various colour schemes and sizes, making them ideal for a bedside table or office desk.

Fidget spinners
Little gadgets known as fidget spinners come in various colours and shapes. The middle finger and thumb hold them at one spot as the other fingers spin them. It may provide a soothing, low-pitched hum and a captivating display of colours. Toys like fidget spinners and others may be useful for focusing attention and calming anxious energy. But, research indicates that it's crucial to use fidget toys sensibly.

Twirly Toys
In that you can twist, flip, and spin the parts without pulling them apart, tangling toys are similar to Rubik's Cubes. These are the perfect toy for young children with ADHD because of their much simpler design. The tangle toys
are physically demanding and aesthetically fascinating because of the colours

and changing shapes.

Pressure Ball
Among the most popular toys for easing anxiety is the stress ball. They come in various shapes and densities and are designed that squeezed between your fingers. The wrist and hand muscles may be contracted and released to possibly have a calming, anti-fidgeting impact. Despite their identity, stress balls probably don't lessen the physiological signs of anxiety or stress.

The Play Dough or Putty
Kids of all ages like playing using slime, putty, or play dough. It is true whether or not they have ADHD. Yet, because of the different sensory experiences and the ability to concentrate and inspire creativity, these toys may be very helpful for those diagnosed. A 2019 research discovered that using "therapy putty" with listening exercises may be very helpful for ADHD kids.

Bubble Poppers for Fidgets
A fidget toy has among the most straightforward designs on the list. It has a pan of fluffy bubbles you push with your fingertips and is often made of soft silicone. It flips over when all bubbles are pushed, allowing you to press them again. It's a great method to reduce anxious energy and soothe agitated hands in order to concentrate or listen quietly intently.

CHAPTER 14

For Home and School Fidgets Objects

14.1 Gaiam Balance Ball Chair

These chairs enable users to tilt, bounce, and roll, all those little motions that support improved focus via physical stimulation—for both children and adults. Also, this chair option is ergonomic and helps your child concentrate. Leg extenders are available for the Balancing Ball Chair, designed to fit standard-sized tables. It is said that the child can work and listen while seated in their chair. Who doesn't want to utilize a bouncer with wheels? Let's face it.

14.2 Twiddle

Twiddle seems to be a real jumble of interconnecting green, purple, and blue components at first sight. Yet, children may bend, move, or flip the linked loop to its fullest and most discrete fidget potential, maintaining them focused and their peers undisturbed. It may even be snapped together or ripped apart. It is compact enough to fit in a pocket yet long enough to wear as a choker or double necklace when unwound. A Twiddle is an item your kid can operate while doing other things.

14.3 Hypercolor Glow

You may manipulate it by stretching, moulding, changing, twisting, and fidgeting. For youngsters who require anything more tactile than a flexible pen and are fascinated with slime, this discreet, non-intrusive fidget works nicely. The green sky hyper colour thinking putty is a unique colour that glows in the dark and changes hue as you play with it from green to blue. Very nice When children have something to do with their hands, children listen better.

14.4 Hokki Stool

Hokki Stools have a height range of between twelve and twenty inches and work on a similar premise to the Balancing Ball Chair. They employ tiny muscle actions to keep your child engaged and on track in class. The chairs, which the business refers to as active sitting, provide movement across all directions, while the cushioned seat prevents slippage. These lightweight stools, which are far more transportable than the balancing chair, come in several sizes, fold for storage, and strengthen the core.

- Strong and at ease
- Encourages youngsters with wiggles to remain still while stationary
- Adaptive design
- Tiny and transportable
- A secure sitting option for kids with certain difficulties

14.5 Balance Disc

This smaller cushion, an active sitting gadget, has a built-in pump and can be inflated to the required hardness. This balance cushion, covered in tiny nubbly bits, aids in enhancing flexibility, coordination, and balance. This incredibly portable fidget encourages active sitting once a little over the price of the Balance Chair & Hokki Stool. It may also be turned over so that it stands. It proved to be the most well-liked educational facility we have.

14.6 Hearos Ear Plugs

Children with ADHD may sometimes need to shut off the outside world, but finding such places at school may be difficult. These covert earplugs may help with that. Musicians choose Hearos earplugs because they are tiny and pleasant to wear for extended periods.

14.7 Tangle Fidget Toy

A sequence of brightly coloured, 90 ° curves which connect and rotate, the Tangle Fidget Toy seems to be the ultimate in silent fidgets. All components could be taken apart or re-used, therefore are meant to be modified and reconstructed into other fidgets for your youngster to discover. Your youngster may use this one-handedly to write, thanks to the soothing, relaxing effect of the curves and twists. Also, compared to other activities like putty, this teacher's favourite is much less messy and produces no noise that might disrupt the class.

14.8 Bouncy Band for Desks

Bouncy bands are now ideal for children who often kick their feet, put them on a seat next to them, or want stimulation from body movement to help them focus. Children may bounce about as they work by using bouncy bands to wrap around the top legs of a typical school desk. The silent bands, a tool for lowering anxiety and hyperactivity, don't bother other kids or instructors. Although many readers hadn't tried them, a few indicated a willingness to do so, particularly in light of their very low price.

14.9 Boinks

Boinks are tiny nylon tubes that have marbles sealed inside of them. To relieve tension or extra energy, rock the marble forth and back. The covert, strong, machine-washable Boinks can also bear forceful bending, pressing, and squeezing.

14.10 Palm Weight

Have a tentative author on your hands? A child that fidgets with their fingers a lot? Try out these wonderful and plush palm weights. Each weight fits snugly into the palm of their hand, is securely fastened with hook-and-loop,
and provides exactly the perfect amount of mechanoreceptors input. Then, as this barely perceptible fidget applies gentle pressure, kids may put their restless fingers to rest.
Everyone, from older children to adults, may use this palm weight using a pencil or pen to write correctly, enhance handwriting, and sharpen writing abilities! Offered in pairs.

• Provides writing with proprioceptive input.
• Stops excessive finger twitching
• Created with Pleasure and Purpose

• Children 3 to 7 can utilize weight on their own.
• The weight may be used while holding a pen or pencil by anybody aged 8 and above.

14.11 Fidget Spinner

In the world of ADHD, fidget spinners were quite popular because they promised to improve focus by providing a place for the user to move about. Both adults and kids used them in meetings and the classroom. Teachers were concerned about distractions in the classroom, while parents wanted their usage to be included in academic planning.

CHAPTER 15

Parents of Children with ADHD Q&A

It might raise many concerns if your kid suffers from ADHD or if you're worried they could. About ADHD there are numerous misconceptions. Knowing what is real and what is false might be challenging.

What Can a Parent Do to Assist Their Hyperactive Child?

Children who have ADHD do best in surroundings that are both structured and adaptable. Also, they do best when they create supportive networks and role models. Nonetheless, your youngster will gain much by speaking up in class and asking questions.

Can the school get a process to support diversity concerns and intervene when necessary?

A youngster with ADHD will have particular problems with other kids. Find out how your school handles certain circumstances to better understand your situation. If you hear processes that you agree with, it may also help you feel more at ease.

Are the arrangements for educating and studying flexible?

Children with ADHD may not always learn in the same manner as other pupils and sometimes need additional pauses. Inquire about flexibility to find out how you and your kid are working. It may aid with managing time and focusing on certain academic issues.

What effects does untreated ADHD have?

A youngster with ADHD may struggle in school and make friends if not treated. Also at risk is family life. Stress between children and their parents due to untreated ADHD might grow. When parents can't connect with their kids, they often blame themselves. It may be incredibly upsetting to feel like you're losing control. Teens with ADHD are more likely to be involved in car accidents. Compared to the general population, adults having untreated ADHD have greater rates of divorce & job loss. Fortunately, there are safe and effective medications that may help adults and children with ADHD manage their symptoms and avoid negative outcomes.

Could a toddler have ADHD?

It is a very good query. Furthermore, it's a hard one. Toddlers tend to be impulsive and busy. Some of them naturally have trouble concentrating. They switch between activities fast. They are dirty, have difficulty waiting, and only pay attention for short periods. In other words, kids could exhibit what we often associate with ADHD symptoms as toddlers.
Yet, this does not imply that toddlers cannot have ADHD. Some very young toddlers are so impulsive and energetic that it raises safety issues. Their outlandish actions could also have an impact on relationships or learning.

Will my kid qualify for Section 504 even though she has ADHD but is not eligible for an IEP?

Maybe. An IDEA-rejected kid can be eligible for coverage through Section 504. The important question is if the student's ADHD significantly affects a vital aspect of their daily lives.

How to make tasks meaningful?

Most of us typically need to be enthusiastic and engaged to finish things. Consider the purpose behind your work. What benefit do you get from it? For instance, you can be driven to work hard because you care deeply about a greater cause or want to save money for a new vehicle or trip. You could be inspired to complete a work for your educational institution by the project's interest or your ambition to graduate. Whatever it is, don't lose sight of the goal.

Where to find an ADHD coach?

ADHD coach may play a crucial role on your treatment team. A coach offers clients skills and tactics to help them reach their objectives and overcome obstacles. Get expert recommendations from psychiatrists or psychologists and inquire about the coach's educational history before hiring them. Look for a degree related to coachings, such as psychology or education.

How to form support groups: Establish contacts and seek assistance.

People who have or are now going through comparable experiences are brought together in support groups.
For instance, this area of overlap may include cancer, persistent illnesses, addiction, grief, or caring.
In a support group, people might discuss their stories, thoughts, coping mechanisms, or direct knowledge of illnesses or treatments. A wellness support group may bridge the gap for many individuals between the need for comfort and support and medical care. A person's relatives and friends might not comprehend the effects of sickness or therapy, and a person's connection with a doctor and other medical professionals might not be able to adequately support them emotionally. A bridge between physical and emotional requirements could be created through a support group of individuals with similar experiences.

Will ADHD alter or become better with time?

Many people's symptoms of ADHD become better with age and experience. Age nearly generally results in less hyperactivity. The most persistent ADHD symptoms are inattentive ones like distractibility and disorganisation. Impulsivity often changes over time. An impulsive adult may struggle with handling finances, making judgements while driving, or speaking before considering their words, unlike an impulsive youngster who would take toys
from classmates or speak out in class before raising their hand. Instead of waiting to observe how the symptoms evolve, it is ideal for creating a care plan for ADHD while your kid is still a young child so you can put them on a road to conquer their obstacles.

CHAPTER 16

Dyslexia, Dyscalculia, Dysgraphia: Different Ways of Learning

16.1 Neurodiversity

Understanding neurodiversity may assist you in shifting the emphasis away from limitations and onto everyone's unique skills.

Approximately 15% of people are estimated to have a neurodiverse personality. The vast majority of people are neurotypical.

Since ADHD is a neurodevelopmental illness, it results from a person's brain growing differently at crucial phases of development earlier than they were born or became a very young kid. It results in symptoms, associated behaviours, and characteristics. It is distinct from mental illness, which describes behavioural patterns in which a person exhibits a "state of mind" dissimilar from their "normal self."

The lack of a real "normal" mental state to compare neurodevelopmental problems makes therapy more challenging since it is impossible to tell whether someone has received treatment. Making ensuring that persons with ADHD may realise their full potential is the aim of ADHD therapy.

Brain training or neurofeedback in children with ADHD

There's no reason to stop taking medicine if you or your kid are considering neu-rofeedback. You may use it whether or not you take medication for ADHD.
Insurance may not always cover it. You may learn more about coverage from your insurance provider and any psychologist or doctor managing your child's ADHD.

Not everyone will like it. It is up to you to determine if it would be a wise choice for yourself or your kid.
That requires time. During many months, there are several weekly visits requi-red. "I advise parents to consider the age at which they, their kids, and themsel-ves can commit. Summer vacation being the best time for many families since they can prioritise it, "affirms Steiner.
An expert is needed for that. Psychologists, nurses, doctors, and other qualified professionals may use neurofeedback.

16.2 Dyslexia

Early intervention is crucial when learning about dyslexia, a prevalent message. Of fact, early diagnosis of any ailment is beneficial. So don't feel bad if you find out your kid has dyslexia later in life. It is not too late to be checked out and re-ceive your needed help.

If your kid has both dyslexia and ADHD, the symptoms of ADHD may obscure the dyslexia warning signals. Also, children often discover strategies to overcome and conceal their troubles, making identifying possible issues more difficult.
You may still have a dyslexia exam if you are studying this while an adult and suspect you may be dyslexic. Knowing what's causing your problems can boost your self-esteem, career, and confidence even if you aren't enrolled in school or a university.

16.3 Signs & Symptoms of Dyscalculia

A diagnostic called dyscalculia is used to identify problems with arithmetic con-cept learning. It's referred to as numerical dyslexia sometimes, although that's a little deceptive. Although dyscalculia is especially connected to mathematics, dyslexia is a term used to describe difficulties with reading and writing. Dyscal-culia encompasses more than just having trouble
comprehending arithmetic. It's more serious than adding numbers incorrectly or writing down the numerals backwards. Dyscalculia makes it challenging to com-

prehend the more general ideas that underpin mathematical principles, such as whether one quantity is larger than the other and how algebra operates.

Learning and recalling mathematical skills are among the characteristics of children with dyscalculia that is most often acknowledged.

The inability to perform arithmetic operations, together with immature problem-solving techniques, lengthy solution periods, and high mistake rates, is the second characteristic of children with dyscalculia.

Furthermore, subitizing and weak number awareness are fundamental deficiencies.

A person's capacity to utilise and comprehend numbers is called number sense. While doing computations, those with a strong number sense are adaptable in their methods and approaches and have a solid understanding of how numbers interact.

The capacity to quickly count an object's number without actually counting it is known as subitizing.

Most individuals may often subitize a maximum of six or seven items. A youngster with dyscalculia, however, could struggle with this and have to count even a modest number of items. When shown two things, for instance, they may number them rather than merely recognise that there are two of them.

Additional dyscalculia symptoms and warning indicators include:

• Inadequate knowledge of the mathematical symbols +, -, and x; or possible confusion with these symbols.
• Having trouble with addition, multiplication, subtraction, and division operations. They may also have trouble understanding the phrases "plus," "add," and "add-together."
• Immature techniques like counting all rather than on. By making 137 dots, followed by 78 dots, and then counting each one, the youngster may figure out 137 + 78.
• Difficulty with multiplication.
• Poor mental computation abilities.
• Have trouble using a calculator because of issues entering variables.
• A failure to recognise patterns
• being unable to generalise.
• Difficulty doing routine activities, such as verifying the change.
• Maintaining scores during games is difficult.
• Directional confusion, or having trouble telling north from south, east from west, and left from right, may occur in children with dyscalculia.
• They could transpose or reverse numerals, such as 63 for 36 and 785 for 875.
• To read an analogue and digital clock, they may require assistance.

• They could struggle to manage their time, be perpetually late, forget time-tables and sequences of previous or future occurrences, or all of the above.
• Youngsters with dyscalculia could have trouble recalling the sequence of events during games or sports or comprehending details.
• Dyscalculic individuals may struggle to understand and retain mathematical ideas, rules, formulas, and sequences.
• They cannot conceive and carry out mathematical operations; they might compute correctly but not comprehend why a method succeeded, making applying their expertise to new situations impossible.
• Severe dyscalculia may result in fear of arithmetic and math-related objects.

Instead of being a symptom of dyscalculia, finger-counting is a common tool to help students acquire effective calculation techniques and memorise arithmetic knowledge. But, chronic finger-counting, especially for often repeated, simple calculations, points to a math issue.

16.4 Learning Strategies That Help on Math

Provide instructions in writing.
Students with ADHD may not remember long-spoken commands. Provide written instructions so that students may refer to them at any time. Students are more likely to finish an assignment on time when they can access instructions.

Employ mnemonics and patterns.
Understanding and remembering mathematical topics are made simpler by learning patterns.
Mnemonics are memory tricks, such as the phrase "don't miss Susie's boat" for recalling long division (divide, subtract, multiply, bring down). Kids with ADHD might concentrate more effectively when arithmetic problems seem simple and quick to solve.

Utilize visual aids and technology to assist with arithmetic.
Children with ADHD might benefit greatly from using charts and graphs to help them recall the steps required for difficult computations.
Students may connect with the content in a variety of ways thanks to computers and smartboards as well. It may impact the transition from short to long memory.
Children like how engaging using a tablet or computer is! Math lessons are made to feel like games thanks to sound effects, graphics, points, and incentives.

Divide instructions into manageable chunks.
For children with ADHD, providing one piece of instruction at a time is beneficial.

It keeps pupils' attention on one task at a time and keeps it there throughout the lesson. Both kids, regardless of ADHD, may benefit from this advice. By breaking down instructions, pupils can better finish activities and respond to directions while giving their full attention one item at a time.

Regularly and early check student work.
As they might not have properly listened to instructions, students experiencing ADHD could require being redirected.
Students find having to retake homework to be highly aggravating. It may add to the widespread issue of homework taking hours daily.
A few minutes after starting a task, check classwork and homework to see whether the student has comprehended the instructions or needs further assistance with the arithmetic.

Provide instances from actual life.
For all students, even those with ADHD, using real-world examples may bring arithmetic ideas to life.
Younger kids may learn fundamental ideas with context by understanding how to tell the time and make change with money, for instance.
For older children, measuring the area of a lawn that has to be mowed or using a liquid that fill containers may be used to teach surface area and volume ideas.

Some Actor And Sports Champions With Dyslexia
In a world where reading and writing are essential, And literacy is seen as a measure of one's potential, There are those who struggle with dyslexia, Whose minds are filled with greatness, despite the dyslexia.
Some of the greatest actors and athletes, Have overcome dyslexia to achieve their feats, Their struggles have made them stronger and more resilient, And their stories inspire us to believe in ourselves and be brilliant.
One such actor is the legendary Tom Cruise, Whose dyslexia has never stopped

him from breaking through, To become one of the most successful and talented actors of our time, His dyslexia only fueled his determination to climb.

Robin Williams
Robin Williams was a beloved actor and comedian, whose dyslexia and ADHD was a part of his life's expedition.
He struggled with reading and writing throughout his school days, but his wit and humor always shone through in so many ways.
Despite his dyslexia, Robin Williams found success, as an actor, comedian, and humanitarian, he was the best, his quick thinking and improvisation skills were unmatched and his performances in films like Dead Poets Society, were superb.
Robin Williams used his dyslexia as a source of inspiration and used his humor and creativity to spark imagination. He showed us that our struggles do not define us, but rather strengthen us and that our unique perspective can make us stand out and thus.
So, let us remember Robin Williams for the joy he brought to our lives and for his perseverance in the face of dyslexia's knives.
 He showed us that with humor, creativity, and determination. We can overcome any obstacle and reach our dreams with dedication.

Muhammad Ali
Muhammad Ali took home a gold medal in the Olympic Games held in Rome. He is known as one of the greatest boxers of all time, but few know of the struggles he faced with dyslexia, a climb, his learning difficulties made reading and writing tough, but his mind was sharp and his spirit even rougher.
As a child, Muhammad struggled with school, his dyslexia made it hard to learn and to follow the rules, but he never let it define him or hold him back, Instead, he focused on his boxing skills and the opponents he would attack.
Muhammad's dyslexia made reading and writing a challenge, but he was determined to make a difference and to challenge, he spoke out against injustice and fought for what he believed in and his legacy as a champion for change will always win.
Despite his dyslexia, Muhammad Ali was a force to be reckoned with, his incredible talent and determination to fight never made him miss.
He inspired millions with his courage and strength and his dyslexia was just a small part of his life, a length.

Kimberley Knightley
Actress Keira Knightley claimed that novelist Jane Austen is much to thank for her professional success.
Due to her dyslexia as a child, Keira Knightley had trouble reading. Still, Emma Thompson's adaptation of Jane Austen's "Sense and Sensibility" motivated the

actress to overcome her difficulties.

Knightley told The Guardian, "My parents handed me a copy of the script Emma had written." I was dyslexic, and she helped me overcome it by telling me that if Emma Thompson couldn't read, she'd ensure she did. As a result, you need to start reading as Emma Thompson will do.

Magic Johnson

Magic Johnson is a legendary athlete, Whose dyslexia never held him back, but instead made him complete, His reading and writing struggles were a daily fight, But he never gave up and pushed through with all his might.

Growing up, Magic found it hard to read and spell, But he never let his dyslexia drag him down to hell, He focused on his basketball skills and worked tirelessly every day, To become one of the greatest players of all time, they say.

Despite his dyslexia, Magic achieved so much, Leading the Los Angeles Lakers to five NBA Championships, as such, And earning himself a place in the basketball Hall of Fame, His dyslexia never defined him, or made him feel ashamed.

Magic's story is one of perseverance and triumph and serves as an inspiration for all those who struggle with dyslexia's crimp, he shows us that dyslexia may make things difficult, but it can never stop us, from achieving our dreams and becoming champions, like Magic Johnson, with a brilliant plus.

16.5 Scientists with Dyscalculia

In a world where numbers reign supreme, where math and logic are revered as kings, there are some who struggle to keep up, who find themselves lost in numerical things.

These are the scientists with dyscalculia, whose minds are filled with brilliant ideas, but who must battle every day, against a foe that can bring them to tears. For them, the world is a constant struggle, a place where numbers refuse to make sense, where equations and formulas can seem like a puzzle and arithmetic can feel like a daunting offense.

But do not underestimate their power, for these scientists with dyscalculia, have a unique perspective and insight that can unlock new ways to conquer academia. They see the world through a different lens and bring a fresh perspective to their field, their struggles have taught them to persevere and find new solutions that have yet to be revealed.

Since dyscalculia has only recently been identified as a specific condition, there is no exhaustive list of historical scientists who have suffered from it. Additionally, most dyscalculia diagnoses are based on modern, standardized tests, which weren't available in the past. However, there are some historical scientists who are thought to have struggled with math or other cognitive skills.

For example, it is believed that the 18th century English mathematician, John von Neumann, may have had some difficulty with short-term memory and attention, which are often associated with dyscalculia.
Additionally, some researchers have suggested that the French mathematician Évariste Galois, who died aged just 20 in 1832, may have suffered from dyscalculia or other cognitive disabilities. However, these diagnoses are based on conjecture and not on definitive historical evidence.

Overall, it is important to note that posthumous diagnoses of cognitive impairment or other medical conditions are difficult to make without direct or indirect documentary evidence. It is therefore important to avoid inappropriately diagnosing or assigning labels to historical scientists based on conjectures or hypotheses not supported by reliable historical sources.

Charles Darwin
Darwin had intense math jealousy. He detested the topic as a college student. Darwin's autobiography states, "I tried mathematics, but I went on very slowly." The wealthy young naturalist even invited a tutor to stay with him at his vacation residence in 1828. During a few trying weeks, Darwin fired the guy.
The work, he said, "was revolting to me," mostly because I couldn't understand the early algebraic concepts. My impatience was quite stupid, and I have since profoundly regretted not having advanced far enough to at least comprehend some of the major founding principles of mathematics. Men with such abilities seem to possess an additional sense.

Thomas Edison
Advanced mathematics was a subject that Edison understood very little about. He thus welcomed a German mathematician named Charles Proteus Steinmetz into the fold after helping to build the General Electric Corporation. Steinmetz, a mathematical prodigy, was responsible for much of G.E.'s technological foundations.

In the past, Edison had employed yet another mathematician, Francis Upton of Bay State, to do calculations that would aid him in performing different lab experiments. Before splitting up in 1911, they collaborated on devices like the watt-hour metre and the incandescent light.

Alexander Graham Bell

The Scottish-born father of the telephone developed a hate-love relationship with arithmetic throughout high school. Robert V. Bruce, Bell's biographer, claims that although Bell "enjoyed the cerebral exercise" of this topic after he grasped the procedure, he became "bored and consequently sloppy in hammering out the ultimate result." In turn, his grades dropped. Bell's mathematical skills never improved and remained below average for a scientist until his death.

CHAPTER 17

The Guide to Solving Disorganization at School

Keeping organised may be difficult for anybody, but it can be particularly difficult for someone with ADHD.

Following ADHD organising techniques may help you restore control if you're overburdened by clutter, tasks, or obligations.

Little changes like maintaining things simple, making lists, and positioning yourself for success are all things that may help.

Recognize that you are not alone. Everyone's demands are different, but many individuals who live with ADHD are seeking for strategies to enhance their organisation.

You may discover an effective method by experimenting with various ADHD organising strategies.

While children who use ADHD medication may demonstrate some improvement in their ability to maintain organisation, they still need help from parents and teachers and instruction in important life skills. Teachers and parents must keep in close contact if they want to help youngsters stay organised.

Give out more goods
If feasible, provide the pupil with 2 sets of resources and books, one for home and a second for school. By doing this, the youngster will have less important information to bring to school daily, freeing up his brain resources for his most

essential task: learning.

Employ the appropriate tools
Employ assignment notebooks with larger-than-normal writing areas for kids with ADHD. A binder with pocket-style inserts for documents may perform better than the typical three-ring binder with tabbed sections if the youngster cram and packs papers in his folders.

Provide written tasks
 If it's not feasible to provide printed directions, ensure the youngster has completed the task and seems to comprehend what he must accomplish at home.
Books and materials should be subject-coloured-coded
For instance, use yellow with all geographic book covers, folders, and notebook dividers. For anything on history lessons, etc., use red.

Create a mechanism for folders that works
Work with the kid to create an organising method which works for him if pupils with ADHD often lose or forget homework while using your conventional folder system. Keep trying and paying attention to the learner; youngsters often have fantastic ideas. It can take some time and experimentation.

CHAPTER 18

Some Winning Behaviors

Whether on purpose or not, you undoubtedly have habits and actions that add unnecessary stress to your life. Given that ADHD tends to cause and even promote certain behaviours, it may not entirely be your fault.

Following are examples of some winning behaviours:

Difficulty #1: Being independent

"Since we have a great deal of self-worth baggage, adults with ADHD are poor delegation skills. We might not feel like we have a right to demand assistance."

Behaviours to have:

1. Consider the work at hand. Consider how you would describe the issue to someone unfamiliar with it. Spend as much time as necessary to outline the problem, including the procedures to fix it, in writing or on tape. It typically clarifies which duties you may begin to assign.

2. Smile as you assign. If you're having problems asking for assistance, consider praising the individual on their skill at doing the work perfectly. In the end, everyone benefits.

Difficulty #2: Lack of Nutrients

"Body and mind are sensitive in those with ADHD. We all know that this is what we eat affects our general functioning, mood, energy, and symptoms. Yet, consistently including nutrient-dense, energetic meals may be tough, particularly when you have poor organisation and planning skills or challenges managing cravings for other foods."

Behaviours to have:
1. Recognize and replace. List the meals and snacks you typically eat for breakfast, dinner, lunch, and snacks. Keep track of all the times you consume meals that don't leave you feeling your best. Try, slowly, substituting a suitable substitute for each meal.
2. Understand your dietary reactions. You could discover that a breakfast high in protein keeps you alert and energetic all day. The same is frequently true for complex carbohydrates, which give out a steady stream of energy since they take longer to digest than simple carbohydrates. Another important factor in feeling energy is staying hydrated.

Difficulty #3: Getting on Your Good

"The main obstacles to action are fear, apathy, and chaos; as a result, we put off taking action and trick ourselves into believing we can't. One of the most prevalent symptoms of ADHD is disarray, which manifests as a lack of direction and paralysis on where and how to begin."

Behaviours to have:
1. The whole image is not necessary. When we wait until we know all the answers once starting, we often freak ourselves out. In any case, take that action to avoid this. With each choice, the following step and the one after it becomes evident.
2. Choose one object, then go on. We are entitled to toss a dart and complete the one job it strikes if it seems hard to prioritise a long list of tasks. Let yourself select one thing nearly at random and then go on.

Difficulty #4: Worrying

The ADHD brain becomes weary and depleted when worried. It consumes limited mental resources and reduces your capacity to embark on a challenging activity when the situation demands it. As the mind spirals, creativity AND problem-solving are likewise blocked.

Behaviours to have:
1. Future events are unpredictable. We spend our energy and time envisioning the unpleasant things and sensations to come unless we formulate remedies

to a foreseen issue.

2. Recall that the past is the past. Nothing you obsess about will make the situation different. Yet, by learning how to move on, we may be able to stop the bad scenario from happening again.

3. Pay attention to your inner voice. Try to recognise when you start worrying, just like you would with negative self-talk. You will be reminded by this one action alone that worrying is a habit of thinking about hypothetical situations. Then, you can try to remedy the issue or just let it go.

CHAPTER 19

Management of ADHD in a Multicultural Society: Navigating Cultural Perspectives and Legal Frameworks

1.7 Significance of Cultural Perspectives

The understanding of cultural perspectives is paramount when examining ADHD management within a multicultural society like the United States. Cultural perspectives encompass a wide range of factors, including beliefs, values, norms, and expectations that shape how a particular society perceives and responds to ADHD. These perspectives influence various aspects of ADHD management, including the recognition of symptoms, help-seeking behaviors, treatment approaches, and the stigma associated with the disorder.

Cultural perspectives play a crucial role in shaping the way individuals, families, and professionals perceive and respond to ADHD symptoms. For example, in some cultures, hyperactivity and impulsivity may be more accepted and considered as normal childhood behavior, leading to a delay in seeking professional help.

Cultural variations can also influence the emphasis placed on academic performance versus behavioral control, impacting the priorities and interventions implemented by parents and educators. Understanding these cultural nuances is vital in developing effective strategies to support children with ADHD and their families.

1.8 Role of Legal Frameworks

The legal framework surrounding ADHD in the United States plays a significant role in shaping the management and support provided to individuals with the disorder. Legislation and regulations establish guidelines for diagnosis, treatment, educational accommodations, and access to mental health services. These legal frameworks aim to ensure that individuals with ADHD receive appropriate support, reasonable accommodations, and access to necessary interventions to optimize their functioning and well-being.

In the American context, several laws protect the rights of individuals with ADHD, including the Individuals with Disabilities Education Act (IDEA), Section 504 of the Rehabilitation Act, and the Americans with Disabilities Act (ADA). These laws mandate the provision of free appropriate public education (FAPE) for students with disabilities, including ADHD, and require schools to create individualized education programs (IEPs) or 504 plans to address their unique needs. Furthermore, these legal frameworks protect individuals with ADHD from discrimination and ensure equal opportunities in various domains of life, such as employment and public services.

Understanding the legal landscape is essential for parents, caregivers, and professionals involved in the management of ADHD. Knowledge of the rights and protections afforded by the law enables individuals to advocate for appropriate accommodations, access necessary services, and navigate the educational and healthcare systems effectively. By considering the legal aspects, it becomes possible to establish a supportive environment that fosters the optimal development and well-being of children with ADHD.

In this chapter, we will explore the impact of cultural perspectives and legal considerations on the management of ADHD in America. By analyzing the variations across different cultures within the country and delving into the legal framework, we can gain in-depth insights into the unique challenges and opportunities that arise in supporting children with ADHD and their families. This knowledge will equip parents, caregivers, and professionals with the necessary tools to develop culturally responsive strategies and navigate the legal landscape effectively, ultimately promoting the well-being and success of children with ADHD in a multicultural society.

Cultural Perspectives on ADHD

2.1 Cultural Influence on Symptom Presentation

Cultural perspectives significantly shape the way ADHD symptoms are recognized and interpreted within different societies. The manifestation and interpretation of symptoms may vary across cultures due to variations in expectations, social norms, and cultural values. For instance, cultures that prioritize discipline and self-control may perceive hyperactivity and impulsivity as more problematic, while cultures emphasizing individual expression and assertiveness may view these traits as more acceptable or even desirable. Understanding these cultural influences is crucial for accurate diagnosis and appropriate intervention.

2.2 Stigma and Mental Health Perception

Stigma surrounding mental health conditions, including ADHD, can vary across cultures. Cultural beliefs, attitudes, and misinformation about mental health can lead to stigmatization and discrimination. In some cultures, there may be a reluctance to acknowledge and seek help for ADHD symptoms due to the fear of being stigmatized or marginalized. Cultural perspectives on mental health can impact help-seeking behaviors, treatment adherence, and the overall well-being of individuals with ADHD. Addressing stigma through education, awareness campaigns, and cultural sensitivity is vital in promoting early intervention and effective management.

2.3 Beliefs, Values, and ADHD Treatment Approaches

Cultural beliefs and values influence the choice of treatment approaches for ADHD. While medication, such as stimulant medications, is commonly prescribed in Western cultures, other cultures may have reservations or preferences for alternative treatments, such as herbal remedies, dietary modifications, or traditional healing practices.
Cultural perspectives may also shape preferences for behavioral interventions, therapeutic modalities, and parental involvement in treatment. Understanding these cultural preferences and incorporating them into ADHD management can enhance treatment engagement and effectiveness.

2.4 Influence of Parenting Styles and Cultural Expectations

Parenting styles and cultural expectations can impact how ADHD is managed within families and educational settings. Cultural norms and parenting styles may influence the level of structure, discipline, and autonomy granted to children with ADHD. For instance, cultures that emphasize obedience and conformity may employ stricter discipline strategies, while cultures promoting independence and self-expression may adopt more flexible approaches. Cultural expectations regarding academic achievement and career success may also influence parental and educational interventions. Recognizing these cultural influences allows for tailored approaches that align with both the child's needs and cultural values.

In summary, cultural perspectives significantly shape the recognition, interpretation, and management of ADHD symptoms. Understanding these influences is essential for accurate diagnosis, effective treatment, and support for individuals with ADHD. Cultural perspectives impact symptom presentation, the perception of mental health, treatment preferences, and parenting approaches. Culturally sensitive approaches that acknowledge and respect diverse cultural perspectives can enhance engagement, adherence, and overall outcomes in managing ADHD across different cultural contexts.

Cross-Cultural Variations in ADHD Management

3.1 Diagnostic Practices and Criteria

Cross-cultural variations exist in the diagnostic practices and criteria used for ADHD. Diagnostic criteria, such as those outlined in the Diagnostic and Statistical Manual of Mental Disorders (DSM-5) or International Classification of Diseases (ICD-11), provide a standardized framework for diagnosis.
However, cultural factors can influence the interpretation and application of these criteria. For example, cultural norms regarding appropriate behavior, attention, and impulsivity may influence the threshold for diagnosing ADHD. Understanding these variations is crucial for accurate and culturally sensitive assessment.

3.2 Access to Healthcare and Services

Access to healthcare and services for ADHD can vary across different cultures and socioeconomic contexts. Disparities may exist in terms of availability, affordability, and cultural appropriateness of services. In some cultures, there may be limited awareness of ADHD, resulting in delays in seeking help or limited access to specialized care.

Socioeconomic factors, such as income, insurance coverage, and geographic location, can further compound these disparities. Addressing these access issues requires targeted efforts to improve awareness, reduce barriers, and provide equitable access to evidence-based interventions.

3.3 Treatment Approaches and Medication Usage

Treatment approaches for ADHD can differ across cultures. While medication, such as stimulant medications (e.g., methylphenidate), is commonly prescribed in many Western countries, other cultures may have concerns or preferences for non-pharmacological interventions. Cultural practices, beliefs, and attitudes toward medication can influence treatment decisions. Some cultures may prioritize behavioral interventions, psychoeducation, or alternative therapies as the primary mode of treatment. Understanding cultural preferences and tailoring treatment approaches can optimize outcomes and treatment adherence.

3.4 Alternative and Complementary Interventions

Cultural variations also extend to the use of alternative and complementary interventions for ADHD. Some cultures may have traditional healing practices, herbal remedies, or dietary modifications that are believed to be effective in managing ADHD symptoms.

These practices may be used alongside or instead of conventional treatments. It is important to engage in open and respectful discussions with families about alternative interventions, ensuring a balanced approach that incorporates evidence-based treatments while respecting cultural beliefs and practices.

3.5 Cultural Competence in ADHD Assessment and Treatment

Cultural competence is essential in ADHD assessment and treatment. Professionals should possess an understanding of cultural nuances, beliefs, and practices related to ADHD. This includes having culturally sensitive assessment tools, knowledge of cultural variations in symptom presentation, and an awareness of cultural factors that may impact treatment adherence and engagement. Culturally competent practices promote effective communication, trust, and collaboration with individuals and families from diverse cultural backgrounds, leading to improved diagnostic accuracy and treatment outcomes.

Recognizing and addressing cross-cultural variations in ADHD management is crucial for providing optimal care to individuals with ADHD. By understanding the cultural factors that influence diagnosis, treatment preferences, access to care, and alternative interventions, professionals can develop culturally responsive approaches.

Collaboration with families, communities, and cultural intermediaries can enhance engagement, reduce disparities, and improve the overall well-being and outcomes for individuals with ADHD across diverse cultural contexts.

Legal Considerations in ADHD Management

4.1 Overview of American Legislation on ADHD

In the United States, several laws and regulations provide legal frameworks for ADHD management and support. The Individuals with Disabilities Education Act (IDEA) ensures that students with disabilities, including ADHD, receive a free appropriate public education (FAPE) tailored to their individual needs. Under IDEA, eligible students may receive accommodations, specialized instruction, and related services through the development of Individualized Education Programs (IEPs) or Section 504 plans. These plans outline the necessary accommodations and supports to address the educational challenges associated with ADHD.

4.2 Individualized Education Programs (IEPs) and 504 Plans

Individualized Education Programs (IEPs) and Section 504 plans are essential components of ADHD management within the educational system. IEPs provide a comprehensive plan outlining the specific goals, accommodations, and support services required to meet the individual needs of students with ADHD. Section 504 plans, on the other hand, ensure that students with disabilities, including ADHD, receive reasonable accommodations and modifications to fully participate in educational activities. These plans can include extended time for assignments, preferential seating, or the provision of assistive technologies to support learning.

4.3 Accommodations in Educational Settings

Legal protections require schools to provide reasonable accommodations and modifications to students with ADHD to ensure their equal access to educational opportunities. Accommodations can include the provision of preferential seating, extended time for assignments or exams, access to note-taking support, or the use of assistive technologies. These accommodations aim to address the specific challenges related to attention, organization, and impulse control, enabling students with ADHD to fully participate and succeed in the educational environment.

4.4 Accessibility of Mental Health Services

Access to mental health services is a critical component of ADHD management. Legal frameworks, such as the Mental Health Parity and Addiction Equity Act (MHPAEA) and the Affordable Care Act (ACA), strive to improve access to mental health services, including diagnosis and treatment for ADHD. These laws require health insurance plans to provide coverage for mental health services on par with coverage for physical health conditions. However, disparities in access and availability of mental health services still exist, particularly in underserved communities or for individuals without adequate insurance coverage.

4.5 Guardianship and Legal Rights

Legal considerations also extend to issues related to guardianship and legal rights of individuals with ADHD. In some cases, individuals with severe impairments due to ADHD may require a legal guardian to make decisions on their behalf. The legal process for establishing guardianship may vary by state, and it is important for families to understand the rights and responsibilities associated with guardianship.

Additionally, individuals with ADHD have legal rights and protections against discrimination under the Americans with Disabilities Act (ADA) and other anti-discrimination laws. These laws ensure equal opportunities and access to employment, public services, and accommodations in various domains of life.

Understanding the legal considerations in ADHD management is crucial for parents, caregivers, and professionals. Familiarity with the laws and regulations pertaining to education, healthcare, and legal rights empowers individuals to advocate for appropriate accommodations, access needed services, and navigate the systems effectively. Collaboration with school personnel, healthcare providers, and legal professionals can ensure that individuals with ADHD receive the support and protections they are entitled to, promoting their overall well-being and success.

Navigating Cultural and Legal Challenges in ADHD Management

5.1 Cultural Competence in ADHD Assessment and Intervention

Cultural competence is essential when navigating the challenges associated with ADHD management across diverse cultural contexts. Professionals should strive to develop cultural competence by gaining knowledge of cultural beliefs, practices, and values relevant to ADHD. This includes understanding the impact of cultural perspectives on symptom presentation, help-seeking behaviors, and treatment preferences. Culturally competent assessment and intervention involve adapting approaches to align with the cultural background and needs of individuals with ADHD and their families. This can include collaborating with cultural intermediaries, employing interpreters if necessary, and engaging in culturally sensitive communication.

5.2 Culturally Responsive Parent and Caregiver Education

Parent and caregiver education play a crucial role in managing ADHD effectively. Providing culturally responsive education ensures that families from diverse cultural backgrounds have access to accurate information about ADHD. Culturally tailored educational materials, workshops, and support groups can help address cultural misconceptions, reduce stigma, and enhance understanding of available treatment options. Culturally responsive education empowers parents and caregivers to actively participate in their child's ADHD management, fostering strong and loving relationships that promote positive outcomes.

5.3 Collaborative Partnerships with Communities and Cultural Intermediaries

Collaborating with communities and cultural intermediaries is essential for successful ADHD management across cultures. Cultural intermediaries, such as community leaders, religious figures, or trusted individuals within specific cultural groups, can play a crucial role in bridging cultural gaps, reducing stigma, and improving engagement with ADHD services. Building strong partnerships with communities facilitates the development and implementation of culturally appropriate strategies, tailoring interventions to specific cultural contexts, and ensuring that services are accessible, acceptable, and effective for diverse populations.

5.4 Advocacy for Equitable Access and Rights

Advocacy is vital in addressing disparities and promoting equitable access to ADHD services and rights. Professionals and organizations can advocate for policies that support equal access to education, healthcare, and mental health services for individuals with ADHD. This includes advocating for adequate funding for ADHD programs, addressing disparities in access to services, and promoting culturally competent practices within healthcare and educational systems. Advocacy efforts can also focus on reducing stigma, raising awareness, and addressing legal barriers that impede individuals with ADHD from fully participating in society.

5.5 Professional Development and Training

Ongoing professional development and training are essential for healthcare providers, educators, and other professionals involved in ADHD management. Training should encompass cultural competence, legal considerations, and evidence-based practices. Professionals need to stay updated on the latest research, treatment approaches, and legal requirements to provide the best care for individuals with ADHD from diverse cultural backgrounds. This includes understanding cultural nuances, legal frameworks, and the impact of cultural factors on assessment, diagnosis, and intervention.

By navigating the cultural and legal challenges inherent in ADHD management, professionals, parents, and caregivers can ensure that individuals with ADHD receive comprehensive and culturally responsive care. Culturally competent approaches that integrate knowledge of cultural perspectives, legal frameworks, and community partnerships promote equitable access, reduce disparities, and foster positive outcomes for individuals with ADHD. Collaborative efforts involving stakeholders from diverse backgrounds can create a supportive environment where all children, regardless of cultural background, can thrive and reach their full potential.

Promoting Cultural Sensitivity and Inclusion in ADHD Support Systems

6.1 Cultural Sensitivity in Educational Settings

Educational settings play a crucial role in supporting students with ADHD. Culturally sensitive practices involve creating inclusive and supportive learning environments that respect and embrace diverse cultural backgrounds. This includes incorporating culturally relevant examples and materials in curricula, considering cultural differences in communication styles and learning preferences, and promoting multicultural understanding and empathy among students. Culturally sensitive schools foster an atmosphere of acceptance, reduce stigma, and promote the academic and social success of students with ADHD from various cultural backgrounds.

6.2 Culturally Responsive Parent-Teacher Collaboration

Effective collaboration between parents and teachers is essential for successful ADHD management. Culturally responsive parent-teacher collaboration involves recognizing and respecting cultural differences, valuing diverse perspectives, and actively involving parents in their child's education. This collaboration should be based on open communication, mutual understanding, and shared decision-making.

Culturally responsive strategies can include providing information in families' preferred languages, accommodating cultural practices in school events and activities, and involving cultural intermediaries or translators to facilitate communication between parents and educators.

6.3 Community Engagement and Support

Engaging the broader community is key to creating a supportive network for individuals with ADHD and their families. Community organizations, cultural centers, and support groups can play a vital role in raising awareness, providing culturally appropriate resources, and offering peer support. Collaborating with community stakeholders helps build a sense of belonging and connectedness for individuals with ADHD and their families. It also strengthens the support system by promoting understanding, reducing stigma, and providing access to culturally relevant services and interventions.

6.4 Professional Diversity and Cultural Representation

Promoting professional diversity and cultural representation within ADHD support systems is essential for effective and culturally sensitive care. Having professionals from diverse cultural backgrounds can help bridge cultural gaps, enhance communication, and provide culturally nuanced perspectives. This includes recruiting and training professionals from underrepresented communities and ensuring that cultural diversity is reflected in leadership positions, educational materials, and outreach efforts. Culturally diverse professionals can serve as role models, advocates, and sources of support, fostering a sense of trust and understanding among individuals with ADHD and their families.

6.5 Research and Knowledge Exchange on Cultural Factors

Further research and knowledge exchange on the impact of cultural factors in ADHD management are crucial for advancing culturally sensitive practices. Research should explore cultural variations in symptom presentation, help-seeking behaviors, and treatment outcomes.

This includes studying the effectiveness of culturally tailored interventions and identifying strategies to reduce disparities in access to care.

Sharing knowledge and best practices through conferences, publications, and professional networks promotes collaboration, encourages innovation, and strengthens the evidence base for culturally sensitive ADHD management.

By promoting cultural sensitivity and inclusion in ADHD support systems, professionals, educators, and communities can create an environment that recognizes and values the diverse cultural backgrounds of individuals with ADHD. Culturally responsive practices in educational settings, parent-teacher collaboration, community engagement, and professional diversity contribute to improved outcomes, reduced disparities, and enhanced overall well-being for individuals with ADHD. Culturally sensitive approaches ensure that all individuals, regardless of their cultural background, receive the support and resources they need to thrive and succeed in managing their ADHD.

Building Cultural Competence in ADHD Professionals

7.1 Importance of Cultural Competence in ADHD

Professionals Cultural competence is a critical skill for professionals involved in ADHD management. Culturally competent professionals possess the knowledge, attitudes, and skills necessary to work effectively with individuals from diverse cultural backgrounds.
Understanding the influence of culture on ADHD symptoms, beliefs, help-seeking behaviors, and treatment preferences enables professionals to provide culturally sensitive and appropriate care. Culturally competent practitioners can establish rapport, build trust, and develop effective treatment plans that align with the cultural values and needs of individuals with ADHD and their families.

7.2 Cultural Competence Training and Education

Training and education play a vital role in building cultural competence among ADHD professionals. Curricula and professional development programs should incorporate cultural competence components that cover cultural diversity, cultural humility, and the impact of culture on ADHD assessment and intervention. This training should include case studies, experiential learning opportunities, and discussions on cultural factors relevant to ADHD. By enhancing professionals' knowledge and understanding of diverse cultural perspectives, training programs facilitate the development of culturally competent practices.

7.3 Self-Reflection and Awareness

Self-reflection and awareness are essential components of cultural competence. Professionals should engage in ongoing self-reflection to identify personal biases, assumptions, and stereotypes that may impact their interactions with individuals from different cultural backgrounds. This introspection helps professionals recognize and address their own cultural blind spots, facilitating more open-minded and empathetic approaches to ADHD management. Building self-awareness also enables professionals to seek continuous learning, expand their cultural knowledge, and adapt their practices to better meet the needs of diverse populations.

7.4 Collaboration and Mentoring

Collaboration and mentoring are valuable strategies for building cultural competence in ADHD professionals. Collaborating with colleagues from diverse backgrounds allows for shared learning experiences, the exchange of perspectives, and the development of cultural insights. Mentoring relationships with experienced professionals who possess cultural competence can provide guidance, support, and opportunities for reflection and growth. Engaging in interdisciplinary collaboration and seeking diverse perspectives enhance professionals' ability to address the cultural complexities inherent in ADHD management.

7.5 Engaging Communities and Cultural Intermediaries

Engaging communities and cultural intermediaries is instrumental in building cultural competence among ADHD professionals. Collaborating with community leaders, cultural organizations, and community-based agencies allows professionals to gain firsthand insights into cultural values, beliefs, and practices related to ADHD. These collaborations foster understanding, build trust, and promote cultural reciprocity. By involving cultural intermediaries as partners and advisors, professionals can ensure that their practices align with community expectations and are sensitive to the needs of individuals with ADHD from diverse cultural backgrounds.

7.6 Continuing Education and Professional Networking

Continuing education and professional networking are vital for maintaining and enhancing cultural competence among ADHD professionals. Professionals should stay abreast of the latest research, best practices, and cultural considerations in ADHD management through participation in conferences, workshops, and seminars.

Networking with colleagues and engaging in professional organizations dedicated to cultural competence and ADHD management provide opportunities for ongoing learning, collaboration, and the exchange of ideas.

Continuous professional development ensures that ADHD professionals are equipped with the knowledge and skills necessary to deliver culturally sensitive care.

By building cultural competence in ADHD professionals, the field can ensure that individuals with ADHD receive the highest quality of care that is tailored to their cultural needs. Cultural competence training, self-reflection, collaboration, and engagement with communities contribute to improved patient-provider relationships, better treatment outcomes, and reduced disparities in ADHD management. Professionals who embrace cultural competence are better equipped to navigate the complexities of culture, deliver culturally sensitive interventions, and promote the well-being and success of individuals with ADHD from diverse cultural backgrounds.

Managing Children with ADHD in the American Context: Tools and Resources for Parents and Educators

This chapter aims to provide parents and educators in the American context with a scientific and academic approach to managing children with ADHD. By exploring the tools and resources available, we can effectively support children with ADHD, enhance their focus and attention, and promote their overall well-being.

Multimodal Treatment Approach

The American medical community recognizes a multimodal treatment approach as the most effective strategy for managing ADHD. This approach typically combines multiple interventions, such as medication, behavioral therapy, and educational support, to address the diverse needs of children with ADHD. Parents and educators play a vital role in implementing and coordinating these interventions.

Educational Accommodations and Support

The Individuals with Disabilities Education Act (IDEA) and Section 504 of the Rehabilitation Act provide legal protections and support for students with ADHD in the American education system. This section explores the specific educational accommodations and support services available, including Individualized Education Programs (IEPs) and Section 504 plans, which outline individualized strategies and interventions to meet the unique needs of students with ADHD.

Behavioral Interventions

Behavioral interventions, such as parent training programs and behavior management techniques, are integral components of managing ADHD in children. This section examines evidence-based behavioral interventions available in the American context, highlighting programs like Parent-Child Interaction Therapy (PCIT) and Positive Parenting Program (Triple P), which equip parents with practical strategies to promote positive behaviors, improve self-regulation, and strengthen parent-child relationships.

Medication

Medication is commonly prescribed as part of the treatment plan for children with ADHD. This section provides an overview of the medication options available, including stimulant and non-stimulant medications, their benefits, potential side effects, and considerations for parents and educators. It emphasizes the importance of working closely with healthcare professionals to determine the most appropriate medication and dosage for each child.

Assistive Technologies

Advancements in technology have led to the development of various assistive technologies that can support children with ADHD. This section explores the use of assistive technologies, such as apps, digital tools, and organizational aids, to enhance organization, time management, and task completion skills. It also addresses considerations for selecting and integrating assistive technologies effectively.

Parent Support Groups and Networks

Parent support groups and networks provide valuable resources and a sense of community for parents navigating the challenges of raising a child with ADHD. This section highlights the importance of connecting with local and national support groups, online forums, and advocacy organizations. It discusses the benefits of peer support, shared experiences, and access to information and resources that can empower parents in their journey.

Conclusion

Managing a child with ADHD can be complex, but with the appropriate tools and resources, parents and educators can provide the necessary support to help children thrive. By understanding the multimodal treatment approach, educational accommodations, behavioral interventions, medication options, assistive technologies, and parent support networks available in the American context, individuals involved in the child's life can collaborate effectively and foster an environment that promotes the child's focus, attention, and overall well-being.

Practical Strategies for Applying Cognitive Behavioral Therapy (CBT) in Managing ADHD in Children

Cognitive Behavioral Therapy (CBT) is a practical and effective approach for managing ADHD symptoms in children. This chapter aims to provide parents, caregivers, and educators with practical strategies derived from CBT principles to help children with ADHD develop skills, cope with challenges, and thrive in various aspects of their lives. By implementing these strategies consistently, children can experience positive changes and improve their overall well-being.

Setting Clear and Realistic Goals

Work with the child to set clear and attainable goals that target specific areas of improvement. Encourage the child to identify their own goals and involve them in the goal-setting process. Break larger goals into smaller, manageable steps to enhance motivation and success. Regularly review and revise goals as the child progresses.

Setting clear and realistic goals is an essential component of Cognitive Behavioral Therapy (CBT) when managing ADHD in children. It helps provide direction, motivation, and a sense of accomplishment for both the child and their support system. Here, we will explore practical strategies for setting goals that are specific, achievable, and tailored to the child's unique needs:

a) Involve the Child: Encourage active participation from the child in the goal-setting process. This involvement fosters a sense of ownership and motivation. Discuss with the child their aspirations, challenges, and areas they would like to improve upon. This collaboration empowers the child and increases their commitment to the goals.

b) Break Goals into Smaller Steps: Large goals can feel overwhelming for children with ADHD, leading to frustration and disengagement. Breaking goals into smaller, manageable steps makes them more attainable. Each step represents a milestone that the child can celebrate, providing a sense of progress and accomplishment.

c) Use SMART Goals: Apply the SMART framework (Specific, Measurable, Achievable, Relevant, Time-bound) to set clear and meaningful goals. For example, instead of a vague goal like "improve focus," a specific and measurable goal could be "maintain focus on a task for 15 minutes without getting distracted, three times a day during homework time, within the next two weeks."

d) Prioritize Goals: Help the child prioritize their goals based on importance and urgency. Addressing goals that have a significant impact on their daily functioning or well-being can improve their overall quality of life. This approach allows the child to focus on specific areas of improvement and prevents overwhelming them with too many goals simultaneously.

e) Regularly Review and Revise Goals: Goals may evolve as the child progresses and gains new skills. It is important to regularly review and revise goals to ensure they remain relevant and aligned with the child's current needs and abilities. Celebrate goal achievements and discuss any necessary adjustments to maintain a sense of progress and keep the child motivated.

f) Provide Support and Encouragement: Support and encouragement play a vital role in helping children with ADHD stay motivated and persevere in pursuing their goals. Offer praise and recognition for their efforts, acknowledge their achievements, and provide constructive feedback when necessary. Regular check-ins and discussions about their progress can help them stay on track and provide opportunities for troubleshooting any challenges they may face.

By implementing these strategies for goal setting, parents, caregivers, and educators can provide children with ADHD a clear roadmap for improvement. Setting goals that are tailored to the child's needs and capabilities, breaking them into manageable steps, and fostering a supportive environment can enhance their sense of agency, boost self-confidence, and lead to tangible progress in managing ADHD symptoms.

Developing Structured Routines

Create structured routines and consistent schedules to provide predictability and organization for the child. Establish consistent wake-up and bedtime routines, meal times, homework schedules, and leisure activities. Use visual aids, such as calendars and schedules, to help the child understand and follow the routine effectively.

Creating structured routines is a practical and effective strategy derived from Cognitive Behavioral Therapy (CBT) principles when managing ADHD in children. Establishing consistent routines provides predictability, organization, and a sense of stability, which can significantly benefit children with ADHD. Let's explore practical approaches to developing structured routines:

a) Establish Consistent Sleep Patterns: Adequate sleep is crucial for children with ADHD as it helps regulate their attention, mood, and overall functioning. Set regular bedtimes and wake-up times to ensure the child gets sufficient rest. Create a calming bedtime routine that includes activities such as reading, taking a warm bath, or practicing relaxation exercises to promote a peaceful transition to sleep.

b) Designate Specific Time Blocks: Allocate specific time blocks for various activities throughout the day. This includes time for homework, meals, physical activity, recreational activities, and relaxation. Clearly communicate and display the schedule visually so that the child can easily understand and follow it.

c) Use Visual Aids and Timers: Visual aids, such as calendars, schedules, and checklists, can serve as valuable tools to support children with ADHD in understanding and adhering to their routines. Use color-coding or symbols to make the visuals more engaging and easier to comprehend. Additionally, set timers or alarms to help the child transition smoothly between activities and manage time effectively.

d) Incorporate Transition Strategies: Children with ADHD often struggle with transitions between tasks or activities. Help ease transitions by implementing transition strategies. This could involve providing verbal reminders or using visual cues to signal upcoming transitions. Encourage the child to finish the current task or wrap up an activity before moving on to the next one.

e) Provide Clear Instructions and Expectations: Clearly communicate instructions and expectations for each activity or task within the routine. Break down tasks into smaller, manageable steps and provide concise and explicit instructions. This clarity helps the child understand what is expected of them and reduces the likelihood of confusion or overwhelm.

f) Encourage Self-Responsibility: As children develop, gradually encourage them to take responsibility for managing their own routines. Foster independence by guiding them to follow the established routines and participate in maintaining their schedules. Teach them self-monitoring skills, such as using checklists or self-reflection, to assess their adherence to the routine and make necessary adjustments.

g) Flexibility and Adaptability: While structure is beneficial, it is important to allow for flexibility and adaptability within routines. Recognize that unexpected events or changes may occur, and provide the child with the necessary tools and strategies to cope with such situations. Help them learn problem-solving skills and adapt their routines when needed.

By implementing structured routines, parents, caregivers, and educators can provide children with ADHD a framework that promotes consistency, organization, and predictability. Structured routines help children manage their time, reduce stress and anxiety, and improve their overall functioning.

By incorporating visual aids, facilitating smooth transitions, setting clear expectations, and fostering self-responsibility, structured routines become practical tools for managing ADHD symptoms and promoting positive outcomes for children with ADHD.

Utilizing Visual Cues and Reminders

Visual cues and reminders are powerful tools to support children with ADHD in staying focused and organized. Implement visual aids, such as checklists, color-coded systems, and visual schedules, to enhance organization and task completion. Use reminders, such as timers or smartphone alarms, to help the child manage time effectively and transition between activities.
Utilizing visual cues and reminders is an effective strategy derived from Cognitive Behavioral Therapy (CBT) principles when managing ADHD in children. Visual aids serve as powerful tools to enhance organization, improve focus, and support memory and task completion. Let's explore practical approaches to utilizing visual cues and reminders:

a) Visual Schedules: Create visual schedules that outline the child's daily activities and routines. Use pictures, symbols, or written descriptions to represent each task or activity. Display the visual schedule in a prominent location, such as a wall or a whiteboard, where the child can easily refer to it. This visual reference helps the child understand the sequence of activities and provides a sense of structure and predictability.

b) Checklists: Provide the child with visual checklists for specific tasks or assignments. Break down tasks into smaller steps and present them in a checklist format. The child can visually track their progress by checking off completed items. This not only helps the child stay organized but also provides a sense of accomplishment as they see their progress.

c) Color-Coding Systems: Implement color-coding systems to enhance organization and categorization. Assign specific colors to different subjects, activities, or materials. For example, using colored folders, notebooks, or labels for different subjects can help the child quickly locate and differentiate their materials. Color-coding can also be applied to calendars, schedules, and other visual aids to enhance clarity and comprehension.

d) Timers and Alarms: Use timers or alarms to support time management and task completion. Set specific time intervals for each task or activity, and use visual or auditory cues to signal when it's time to transition or move on to the next task. Timers can help the child develop a better understanding of time and improve their ability to gauge the duration of activities.

e) Visual Organization Systems: Create visually organized spaces to help the child maintain order and reduce clutter. Use labeled bins, shelves, or containers to store and categorize items. Clear visuals help the child easily identify where things belong and facilitate independent organization and retrieval of materials.

f) Environmental Reminders: Place visual reminders in the environment to prompt specific behaviors or routines. For example, posting a checklist near the door can remind the child to pack their backpack with necessary items before leaving for school. Visual cues can also be used to remind the child to follow specific routines or engage in desired behaviors, such as washing hands or completing homework.

g) Personalized Visual Supports: Tailor visual cues and reminders to the child's individual needs and preferences. Take into account their learning style, sensory preferences, and strengths when designing visual supports. Involve the child in creating or selecting visuals that resonate with them, as this increases engagement and buy-in.

Consistently utilizing visual cues and reminders helps children with ADHD stay organized, focused, and on-task. By incorporating visual schedules, checklists, color-coding systems, timers, and personalized visual supports, parents, caregivers, and educators can provide children with effective tools to navigate daily routines and manage their responsibilities. Visual cues promote independence, reduce reliance on verbal instructions, and support the child's overall functioning in various settings.

Teaching Self-Monitoring and Self-Reflection

Encourage the child to develop self-awareness by teaching self-monitoring and self-reflection techniques. Help them recognize and identify their own thoughts, emotions, and behaviors associated with ADHD symptoms. Encourage journaling, mindfulness exercises, and regular check-ins to promote self-reflection and self-regulation.

Encouraging self-regulation and executive functioning skills is an essential component of managing ADHD in children. These skills help children develop the ability to control their impulses, organize tasks, prioritize activities, and manage their time effectively. Let's explore practical approaches to encouraging self-regulation and executive functioning skills:

a) Self-Awareness and Reflection: Help children develop self-awareness by encouraging them to reflect on their thoughts, emotions, and behaviors. Teach them to recognize when they are experiencing difficulty with attention, impulse control, or organization. Foster an open and non-judgmental environment where the child feels comfortable discussing their challenges and brainstorming strategies to address them.

b) Mindfulness and Relaxation Techniques: Introduce mindfulness and relaxation techniques to help children improve their focus, attention, and self-regulation skills. Teach them deep breathing exercises, guided imagery, or progressive muscle relaxation. Encourage regular practice of these techniques to promote a calm and centered state of mind, which can positively impact their executive functioning abilities.

c) Task Chunking and Time Management: Break down tasks into smaller, more manageable chunks to help children with ADHD approach their responsibilities effectively. Teach them how to prioritize tasks and allocate appropriate time for each. Utilize visual aids, such as timers or schedules, to help children understand the passage of time and stay on track.

d) Organization and Planning Strategies: Teach children organization and planning strategies to enhance their executive functioning skills. This includes techniques such as using checklists, creating to-do lists, maintaining a calendar, and utilizing organizational tools like folders or binders. Help them develop strategies for organizing materials, setting goals, and planning their activities.

e) Metacognitive Strategies: Encourage metacognitive thinking by teaching children to monitor and evaluate their own thoughts and actions. Help them recognize when they are losing focus or becoming distracted and guide them in implementing strategies to regain attention. Teach them to ask themselves questions like, "Am I on track?" or "Do I understand what I need to do?"

f) Problem-Solving and Decision-Making: Foster problem-solving and decision-making skills to support children with ADHD in navigating challenges and making appropriate choices. Teach them to identify problems, brainstorm potential solutions, consider the consequences of each option, and make informed decisions. Encourage them to reflect on the outcomes and learn from their experiences.

g) Flexibility and Adaptability: Recognize that flexibility and adaptability are important skills for children with ADHD. Help them develop strategies to manage unexpected changes or transitions effectively. Teach them how to adjust their plans or strategies when necessary and embrace new situations with resilience and a positive mindset.

h) Collaborate with School and Support Professionals: Work collaboratively with teachers, school staff, and support professionals to reinforce self-regulation and executive functioning skills. Share strategies and interventions that are effective at home, and seek their input and expertise to support the child's development in the school environment. Consistency between home and school settings can enhance the child's progress and overall success.

By encouraging self-regulation and executive functioning skills, parents, caregivers, and educators empower children with ADHD to take control of their actions and enhance their overall functioning.

Through self-awareness, mindfulness, task chunking, organization, metacognitive strategies, problem-solving, and collaboration, children can develop important skills to manage their ADHD symptoms and thrive in various aspects of their lives. The cultivation of these skills not only improves their academic performance but also fosters resilience, independence, and long-term success.

Developing Effective Communication and Positive Parenting Strategies

Developing effective communication and positive parenting strategies is essential in managing ADHD in children. These strategies can help establish clear expectations, maintain consistent routines, and foster a supportive and nurturing environment. Let's explore practical approaches to developing effective communication and positive parenting strategies:

a) Clear and Consistent Expectations: Establish clear and consistent expectations for behavior, routines, and responsibilities. Clearly communicate these expectations to the child, using simple and concise language. Reinforce positive behavior and provide specific feedback when expectations are met. Consistency in expectations helps children with ADHD understand boundaries and promotes a sense of structure and predictability.

b) Active Listening and Empathy: Practice active listening and empathy when communicating with your child. Show genuine interest in their thoughts, feelings, and experiences. Validate their emotions and provide a supportive environment where they feel heard and understood. This can enhance the parent-child relationship and facilitate effective communication.

c) Positive Reinforcement: Utilize positive reinforcement techniques to encourage desired behavior and achievements. Offer praise, rewards, or incentives for completing tasks, demonstrating self-control, or making progress. Positive reinforcement enhances motivation and self-esteem, and it reinforces the child's understanding of what behaviors are expected and valued.

d) Effective Discipline Strategies: Implement effective discipline strategies that focus on teaching and guiding rather than punishment. Use logical consequences that are related to the child's behavior, allowing them to learn from their actions. Set clear boundaries and consistent consequences, providing structure and helping the child develop self-discipline.

e) Break Tasks into Manageable Steps: Break down tasks into smaller, manageable steps to help the child with ADHD approach them more effectively. Provide clear instructions and guide them through each step, offering support and encouragement. This approach promotes success and prevents overwhelming feelings that can lead to inattention or avoidance.

f) Time for Emotional Connection: Set aside dedicated time for emotional connection with your child. Engage in activities they enjoy, such as playing games, reading together, or simply having meaningful conversations. These moments of connection strengthen the parent-child bond, foster emotional well-being, and create opportunities for open communication.

g) Conflict Resolution and Problem-Solving: Teach your child effective conflict resolution and problem-solving skills. Encourage them to express their feelings and opinions respectfully, and guide them in finding solutions to conflicts or challenges. Engage in collaborative problem-solving discussions, where both parent and child contribute ideas and work towards mutually beneficial solutions.

h) Model Self-Regulation and Coping Strategies: Be a positive role model by demonstrating self-regulation and coping strategies. Show your child how to manage stress, regulate emotions, and handle challenges effectively. Use language that reflects problem-solving and positive self-talk, and openly share your own strategies for self-regulation.

i) Seek Support and Self-Care: Recognize the importance of seeking support and practicing self-care as a parent or caregiver. Join support groups, seek professional guidance, and engage in activities that help you recharge and maintain your well-being. Taking care of yourself allows you to better support your child with ADHD.

Effective communication and positive parenting strategies create a nurturing and supportive environment for children with ADHD. Clear expectations, active listening, positive reinforcement, and effective discipline techniques promote understanding and cooperation. Breaking tasks into manageable steps, dedicating time for emotional connection, and teaching conflict resolution skills empower the child's growth and development.

Modeling self-regulation and seeking support and self-care as a parent further enhance your ability to provide the support your child needs. By implementing these strategies consistently, parents and caregivers can strengthen their relationship with their child, promote their well-being, and facilitate their success in managing ADHD.

Implementing Behavior Management Strategies

Use behavior management strategies to reinforce positive behaviors and discourage negative behaviors. Establish clear rules, expectations, and consequences in collaboration with the child. Implement reward systems, such as token economies or sticker charts, to motivate and reinforce desired behaviors. Consistency and immediate reinforcement are key to the effectiveness of these strategies.

Implementing behavior management strategies is a crucial aspect of managing ADHD in children and is rooted in Cognitive Behavioral Therapy (CBT) principles. These strategies help children develop self-control, regulate their behavior, and improve their ability to make positive choices. Let's explore practical approaches to implementing behavior management strategies:

a) Clear and Consistent Expectations: Establish clear and consistent expectations for behavior. Communicate these expectations explicitly to the child and ensure they understand what is expected of them. Use simple and concrete language to outline the desired behaviors and provide examples when necessary. Reinforce these expectations consistently across different settings and contexts.

b) Positive Reinforcement: Utilize positive reinforcement to encourage and reinforce desired behaviors. Offer praise, rewards, or privileges when the child demonstrates appropriate behavior. This can include verbal praise, stickers, tokens, or a reward system where the child earns points toward a larger reward. Positive reinforcement helps motivate the child, increase their self-esteem, and strengthen positive behavior patterns.

c) Behavior Contracts: Implement behavior contracts as a collaborative tool between the child, parents, and teachers. A behavior contract outlines specific behavioral expectations, consequences for inappropriate behavior, and rewards for meeting the desired goals. Involve the child in the process of creating the contract to enhance their sense of ownership and commitment.

d) Token Economy Systems: A token economy system involves giving the child tokens or points for demonstrating desired behaviors. These tokens can be exchanged for predetermined rewards or privileges. This system provides a visual representation of progress and helps children understand the connection between their behavior and rewards. It also encourages consistency and reinforces positive behavior over time.

e) Time-Out and Cool-Down Strategies: Time-out and cool-down strategies can be effective for managing impulsive or disruptive behavior. Establish a designated time-out area or space where the child can take a break and calm down when needed. Use a calm and neutral tone when implementing time-outs, focusing on providing the child an opportunity to self-regulate and reflect on their behavior.

f) Behavior Tracking and Self-Monitoring: Track the child's behavior using behavior charts or logs to identify patterns, triggers, and progress. Involve the child in self-monitoring their behavior by encouraging them to track their own actions and reflect on their choices. This self-awareness helps the child develop insight into their behavior and empowers them to make positive changes.

g) Teach Coping Skills and Problem-Solving: Teach the child coping skills and problem-solving techniques to manage impulsive or challenging situations. This can include deep breathing exercises, using self-talk to redirect attention, or taking a break to calm down. Provide guidance and practice opportunities for the child to develop these skills and apply them in real-life situations.

h) Consistency and Collaboration: Consistency is key when implementing behavior management strategies. Ensure that parents, caregivers, and teachers are aligned in their approach and consistently reinforce expectations and consequences. Collaborate with educators to establish consistent strategies and reinforce positive behavior across home and school settings.

By implementing these behavior management strategies, parents, caregivers, and educators can help children with ADHD develop self-control, regulate their behavior, and make positive choices. Clear expectations, positive reinforcement, behavior contracts, and token economy systems create a structured framework that promotes positive behavior patterns.
Time-out and cool-down strategies, behavior tracking, coping skills, and problem-solving techniques equip children with the tools to manage their impulses and navigate challenging situations. Consistency and collaboration across home and school settings maximize the effectiveness of these strategies and support the child's overall development.

Promoting Healthy Lifestyle Habits:

Promoting healthy lifestyle habits is a crucial aspect of managing ADHD in children. A healthy lifestyle can positively impact their overall well-being, reduce symptom severity, and improve their ability to focus and regulate their behavior. Let's explore practical approaches to promoting healthy lifestyle habits:

a) Balanced Diet: Encourage a balanced diet that includes a variety of nutritious foods. Limit processed foods, sugary snacks, and beverages high in caffeine. Provide regular meals and snacks that contain protein, complex carbohydrates, and healthy fats, which can help stabilize blood sugar levels and support brain function.

b) Regular Physical Activity: Promote regular physical activity as part of the child's routine. Engage them in activities they enjoy, such as sports, dance, biking, or swimming. Physical exercise helps release excess energy, improves mood, and enhances concentration and cognitive function.

c) Sufficient Sleep: Ensure the child gets sufficient sleep based on their age and individual needs. Establish consistent bedtime routines and create a conducive sleep environment that is quiet, dark, and comfortable. Adequate sleep supports cognitive functioning, attention, and emotional regulation.

d) Minimizing Screen Time: Set limits on screen time and encourage alternative activities that promote engagement, creativity, and social interaction. Excessive screen time can contribute to inattention and hyperactivity. Encourage outdoor play, reading, hobbies, and family activities as healthy alternatives.

e) Stress Management Techniques: Teach the child stress management techniques to help them cope with the challenges of ADHD. This can include deep breathing exercises, mindfulness, relaxation techniques, or engaging in activities they find calming or enjoyable. Encourage open communication and provide a supportive environment to help them navigate stressors effectively.

f) Social Support and Positive Relationships: Foster positive relationships and social support for the child. Encourage them to engage in social activities, join clubs or groups, and participate in extracurricular activities that align with their interests. Positive relationships contribute to emotional well-being and provide a sense of belonging.

g) Educating and Empowering the Child: Educate the child about ADHD and empower them to take an active role in managing their condition. Teach them about their strengths, challenges, and the strategies available to help them succeed. Encourage them to advocate for themselves, communicate their needs, and seek support when necessary.

h) Parental Self-Care: Recognize the importance of parental self-care in managing ADHD in children. Parents and caregivers need to prioritize their physical and emotional well-being. Take time for self-care activities, seek support from others, and practice stress management techniques. When parents are well-rested and emotionally balanced, they can better support their child's needs.

By promoting healthy lifestyle habits, parents, caregivers, and educators provide a supportive foundation for children with ADHD. A balanced diet, regular physical activity, sufficient sleep, limited screen time, stress management techniques, social support, and parental self-care contribute to overall well-being and symptom management. These habits support the child's ability to regulate their behavior, maintain focus, and enhance their overall quality of life.

Collaborating with Professionals and Support Systems:

Collaborating with professionals and utilizing support systems is a vital aspect of managing ADHD in children. Seeking guidance from experts and engaging in a collaborative approach can provide valuable resources, interventions, and strategies to support the child's development. Let's explore practical approaches to collaborating with professionals and support systems:

a) Consultation with Mental Health Professionals: Consult with mental health professionals, such as psychologists, psychiatrists, or behavioral therapists, who specialize in ADHD. They can provide a comprehensive assessment, diagnosis, and treatment recommendations tailored to the child's specific needs. Collaborate with these professionals to develop an individualized treatment plan and discuss therapeutic interventions.

b) Individualized Education Program (IEP) or 504 Plan: If the child attends a school in the United States, work with the school's special education team to develop an Individualized Education Program (IEP) or a 504 Plan. These plans outline accommodations, modifications, and support services necessary to meet the child's educational needs. Collaborate with teachers and school staff to ensure consistent implementation of the plan.

c) Parent Training and Education Programs: Attend parent training and education programs specifically designed for parents of children with ADHD. These programs provide valuable information, strategies, and support networks. They empower parents with knowledge and skills to effectively manage their child's ADHD, navigate challenges, and promote their child's success.

d) Support Groups and Communities: Seek out support groups or communities that focus on ADHD. These groups provide a platform for parents, caregivers, and children to connect, share experiences, and gain support from others who understand the challenges associated with ADHD. Participating in such groups can provide emotional support, practical advice, and a sense of belonging.

e) Collaboration with Teachers and School Personnel: Maintain open and regular communication with teachers and school personnel to ensure a collaborative approach to managing ADHD in the educational setting. Share information about the child's strengths, challenges, and effective strategies. Work together to implement accommodations, modifications, and behavioral interventions that support the child's academic and social development.

f) Utilizing Technology and Apps: Explore technology-based tools and apps specifically designed to assist children with ADHD. These resources can help with organization, time management, task reminders, and focus enhancement. Collaborate with professionals and educators to identify suitable apps or technologies that align with the child's needs.

g) Multi-Disciplinary Approach: Embrace a multi-disciplinary approach by involving various professionals, such as occupational therapists, speech therapists, or social workers, depending on the specific needs of the child. Collaborate with these professionals to integrate their expertise and interventions into the child's treatment plan.

h) Regular Monitoring and Adjustments: Continuously monitor the child's progress and make necessary adjustments to interventions and strategies. Collaborate with professionals, educators, and support systems to assess the effectiveness of the implemented approaches and modify them as needed. Regular communication and feedback loops ensure ongoing support and optimize outcomes.

By collaborating with professionals and support systems, parents, caregivers, and educators can access valuable expertise, interventions, and resources to effectively manage ADHD in children. Consultation with mental health professionals, involvement in individualized education programs, and participation in parent training programs empower parents and caregivers with knowledge and support.

Engagement in support groups and collaboration with teachers, school personnel, and other professionals create a comprehensive network of support. Utilizing technology and embracing a multi-disciplinary approach further enhance the child's overall management and well-being. Regular monitoring and adjustments ensure that interventions remain effective and tailored to the child's evolving needs.

Conclusion

Due to the stigmatising views of family and community members, parents of children with ADHD face stress while they try to manage the child's symptoms. Parents struggle with heavy emotions and poor social and professional performance. In addition to providing multidisciplinary treatments to educate and support families of children with ADHD, healthcare professionals must be aware of the difficulties of raising such a kid.

It cannot be disputed that a growing number of children with ADHD were receiving the correct diagnosis and treatment. Yet, more has to be taken to ensure that all children with this condition benefit from a modern strategy for overcoming their difficulties. For this to happen, there must be a broad change in how people see children with behavioural, emotional, and educational difficulties. We must quit criticizing kids and their loved ones for their behavioural and academic difficulties as soon as possible.

We must understand that thought, self-worth, conduct, and emotion all originate in the brain. We need to be open to the possibility that many of the problems kids face have something to do with their brains. We should treat ADHD with the same seriousness with which we currently handle conditions like asthma and diabetes. As a consequence of these achievements, many more kids will have the opportunity to see a future full of pleasure and satisfaction.

As we come to the end of this journey together, I want to take a moment to express my deepest gratitude to you for joining me on this mission to raise happy, successful kids with ADHD. I hope that the practical tips and advice provided in this book have helped you better understand your child's condition and given you the tools to help them thrive.

Parenting a child with ADHD can be a challenging experience, but it can also be incredibly rewarding. By learning more about your child's unique needs and working together with them to create a supportive environment, you can help them reach their full potential and achieve their dreams.

Remember, your child is not defined by their ADHD. They are a wonderful, complex individual with their own strengths, weaknesses, and interests. By focusing on their strengths and helping them to build skills in areas where they may struggle, you can help them to develop a strong sense of self-worth and confidence.
I hope that this book has provided you with some practical strategies and tools to help you on this journey.
Whether it's creating a consistent routine, setting up a supportive homework environment, or engaging in positive reinforcement techniques, there are many ways that you can help your child to succeed.
As we close this chapter, I want to remind you that You Are Not Alone. There are many resources available to you, from support groups and online forums to therapy and coaching. Don't hesitate to reach out for help and guidance whenever you need it.

If you found this book helpful, I would greatly appreciate if you could leave a positive review on Amazon. Your feedback will not only help other parents find this valuable resource, but it will also encourage our team to continue producing high-quality content.

Thank You for the Support, and me and my Team Wish You All The Best In Your Parenting Journey.

Sincerely,

Grace S. Anderson